Harmful Religion

Harmful Religion

AN EXPLORATION OF RELIGIOUS ABUSE

Edited by Lawrence Osborn
and Andrew Walker

First published in Great Britain 1997
Society for Promoting Christian Knowledge
Holy Trinity Church
Marylebone Road
London NW1 4DU

British Library Cataloguing-in-Publication Data
A catalogue record of this book is available from the British
Library.

ISBN 0-281-04936-X

Typeset by Simon Jenkins Associates
Printed in Great Britain by The Cromwell Press,
Melksham, Wiltshire

Contents

Contents

Foreword

This book, with the exception of Professor Rubin's chapter, is a collection of papers first read at a conference on harmful religion at the Centre of Theology and Culture, King's College, London. The conference was attended by over 200 each day and was extensively covered by the broadsheets as well as the religious press.

The King's conference was billed as 'an exploration' into harmful religion and this was to highlight the tentative and controversial nature of the subject matter. We thought it better to open the exploration of this important issue with an open debate from scholars and care practitioners rather than assume that we had already successfully delineated the field, defined the problem, or come to a consensus on the nature of harmful religion and how to combat it.

It follows, therefore, that this book, reflecting as it does the King's conference, does not pretend to represent a particular viewpoint. The papers do not necessarily reflect our view or agree with each other. We would like, however, to highlight two issues which do reflect our concerns as editors. First, we have avoided the temptation to view harmful religion as the exclusive provenance of the cults. Not only are cults dubious sociological categories, but their emotive connotations might seem to suggest that cults are always bad for you, while mainline religion is good for you or at least harmless. We think that it does not always follow that cults are necessarily harmful if measured in terms of physical, emotional and psychological abuse.

Conversely, we do not think that it follows that mainline Christianity is exempt from the problems of religious abuse. On the contrary, we believe that the whole debate on harmful religion has been skewed by seeing it as a problem of cults, to the extent that long-standing denominations and established sects have escaped careful scrutiny. In this respect, this book represents an attempt to put the churches under the microscope rather than the more esoteric and syncretistic cults.

Our second concern is a Christian one. Both of us are theologians concerned with the promotion of historic orthodoxy in contemporary culture. Between us, in our writings, we have highlighted the problems of New Age religion, modernist and postmodernist theology. In the course of this work, however, we have discovered that our Christian commitment has to be tempered by the fact that empirically the churches do not always promote good religion either in terms of beliefs or practices.

This is clearly an issue of public interest for all those committed to good citizenship and moral values, but it is also of particular concern for the Christian who believes that the gospel is good news for humankind. It is in the light of the gospel that we feel constrained to say that religion can be bad for you.

Lawrence Osborn, Ridley College, Cambridge
Andrew Walker, King's College, London

Introduction

Exploring Harmful Religion
Andrew Walker

One of the silliest things I have ever heard was President Eisenhower's insistence that America should be driven by religion – although he did not care which religion it was! And yet such a view is no laughing matter, for religion in itself is blatantly not good for us. Religion can mean human sacrifice to Moloch, as well as self-sacrifice. It can legitimate war and genocide, as well as sanction the moral values of a civilized society.

The history of Christianity in particular, we need to remind ourselves, is one of murder as well as martyrdom. If historically it stood for the truth against what FitzSimmons Allison has called 'the cruelty of heresy',[1] it has often done so by being wickedly cruel to heretics. The modern world is arguably less blighted by such witch-hunting, yet we are no more free from Christian religious wars and terrorist activity than we were in the Middle Ages. In former Yugoslavia we see Catholic Croatians and Serbian Orthodox engaging in the 'ethnic cleansing' of each other. Northern Ireland still bears the seeping scars of Protestant and Catholic tribal hatred, while in the United States, millennial militias seem prepared to bomb middle America into Armageddon.

When we turn our attention away from the international front to the home front we find, so often, that in the apparent cosiness of our local churches trouble abounds. Of course we know about the 'besetting sins' of church life – backbiting in the choir, jealousy of the new minister, flagrant hypocrisy, the 'filthy rags' of self-righteousness. We are more reluctant, however, to explore the darker issues of how our churches relate to the power structures of the secular world, or how our leaders sometimes harm their flocks rather than feed them. Recent revelations in Catholic Ireland demonstrate that harmfulness may extend to priests sexually

1

molesting young children. Some would say that harm has also been caused through a 'cover-up' (or at least an unacceptable complacency) by the authorities.

The story which broke in the summer of 1995 of Anglican priest Chris Brain and the Nine O' Clock Service at Sheffield is not only one of sexual abuse and religious harm, but also appears to be one of myopia by the diocese.[2] The authorities cannot of course be blamed for not knowing of the sexual misdemeanours, but leading evangelicals have suggested that they did seem curiously unconcerned at the theological deviancy of a 'creation spirituality' that admittedly has its supporters – and possibly even a home in St James Piccadilly – but would seem out of place in a diocese under a conservative bishop.

Such a criticism, however, needs to be balanced by other considerations. Charismatic evangelicals may consider the influence of Matthew Fox to be unhelpful, but things were already going wrong in the Nine O'Clock Service when it was still under the influence of charismatic John Wimber.[3] It simply will not do to suggest that things were fine at St Thomas Crooks when it was charismatic, but became dangerously out of control when it turned to creation spirituality.

It could also be argued, in defence of the diocese, that the Sheffield authorities did not wish to interfere with religious freedom. They had tolerated the Wimber 'clinics', watched with guarded interest the new directions in experimental liturgy, and when Mr Fox arrived on the scene they may have found his approach unorthodox, but he was by the time of his second visit no longer a lay outsider but an ordained Episcopalian priest. With hindsight, it is easy to point the finger at the Sheffield diocese, but myopia is not the same as culpability or synonymous with a 'cover-up'. A more serious question to be raised, as has been by the Venerable George Cassidy, the Archdeacon of the London Diocese, is whether the refusal by the Church of England to hold a formal enquiry into the affair is not tantamount to ignoring the suffering of the young people who experienced abuse at the hands of one of its ordained priests.[4] Certainly it was the case that some of the abused women in the Nine O'Clock Service felt betrayed by the church authorities.[5]

The Sheffield story also reminds us that even if the response of evangelicals to Matthew Fox may not have been accurate in relation to the harmfulness allegedly caused by Chris Brain, they may rightly have been concerned with Fox's theology. The idea that theological deviancy might be harmful makes no sense, of course, unless people are still committed to the idea that Christian truth promotes freedom and liberation but heresy leaves humankind bound up in chains. Lawrence Osborn (in chapter 10) demonstrates that there is a right use of the concept of heresy as well as an all too obvious abuse of it as a mask for naked power.

However, the idea of heresy is often promoted as beneficial rather than harmful, because it seems to suggest a tilt at conventional wisdom or dead tradition.[6] But perhaps bad theology can have undesirable consequences. The British Council of Churches Study Guide on the *Forgotten Trinity*[7] argues that a misshapen theology can cause harm. It claims that a lop-sided doctrine of the Trinity may produce a repressive patriarchy (too much Father), a charismatic triumphalism (too much Spirit), or even a sloppy sentimentality that trivializes the sacred (too much Son).

There is much to recommend in this approach from a traditional Christian perspective, but unfortunately there is no isomorphic relationship between orthodoxy and orthopraxis. An academically or ecclesially correct theology without a living spirituality can itself degenerate into legalism and, in C.S. Lewis's words, 'reverence itself did harm'. Just as antinomianism probably leads to moral turpitude, so the imposition of good theology, in interfering with human dignity and freedom, probably leads to religious abuse.

The addiction model of abuse

But what do we mean when we talk of religion itself being harmful or abusive? In recent years, two models of 'religious harm' which merit serious attention have begun to emerge from the United States. First there is what we might call the addiction model. After the fall-out from the televangelist scandals of the late 1980s, it was observed by many medical and pyscho-social support groups that people were exhibiting all the traits of dependent personalities more usually associated with gambling and alcoholic addiction. A number of self-help groups, including Fundamentalists Anonymous, were set up to provide a support network based on the Alcoholics Anonymous twelve-step programme. Some of the alleged symptoms of this religious addiction were:

• Compulsive and excessive church attendance.
• Inability to think, doubt or question authority.
• Inability of individuals to work things out for themselves.
• Shame-based belief that you are not good enough for God or that you cannot do things right.
• A magical world-view in which God will fix everything for you.

The addiction model needs to be taken seriously. Recently a priest wrote to me saying that while he had to work hard to make some people come to church, there were others that he had to wean off it so that they could get on with their lives. 'Using' religion, like using drugs, is a substitute for coping with real life and a toxin in the spiritual bloodstream. When this happens, church becomes not a place of sanctuary but a retreat from reality; a source of sickness rather than healing; a place of addiction rather than abundance.

There is, in short, much to commend the addiction model, for we know that it fits pastoral as well as clinical experience and it allows us to extend it to the co-dependency of whole families, if not congregations. There are, however, two things about it which should make us cautious of its legitimate application.

First, this is a model much loved by theological liberals, who tend to equate addictive religion with fundamentalist or conservative Christianity. Leo Booth's book, *When God Becomes a Drug*, is an example of this approach.[8] His solution to religious addiction is a course of therapy, the setting-up of a support group, and the gradual transposition of 'closed' religion to an open-ended approach. Does Leo Booth think, we might wonder, that political correctness causes harm? Can a liberal agenda abuse when it is imposed illiberally (see Alan Torrance's experience in chapter 6 of this book)? May a liberal gospel itself be harmful if it promises false hopes or makes false claims (or even false apologies, as David Martin insists in chapter 8)? When religious lay people ask priests for spiritual support and they are given therapeutic prescriptions, what will be the effects of these medicinal approaches: the loss of faith as well as an end to addiction?

Second, as useful as the addiction model may be in some cases, it runs the risk of turning the spotlight of religious abuse onto the individual lay person as victim and away from the abusers – priests, elders, those invested with authority, or those who simply take authority upon themselves. If the co-dependency model of addiction holds true, it does so more often than not because people wittingly or unwittingly are manipulated by those in authority over them. This being so, let us look at the second model of harmful religion to come out of America, and the one that informs this book. This model concentrates on the abuse of power and the misuse of authority.

Harmful religion as the abuse of power

This model has three features to recommend it. First, it is consonant with a thoroughly Christian theology. When Tom Smail, Nigel Wright and I held our workshops in Britain on the charismatic movement, we did so under the rubric of 'the love of power and the power of love'. We were at pains to stress the vulnerable and sacrificial nature of Christian discipleship over and above triumphalism, messianic delusion, rank power. We wanted to show that the Christian way is always the way of the cross, of service and servanthood.[9]

Not that obsession with, and the abuse of, power is by any means an exclusive charismatic temptation. It is the way of the Devil, who wants to become God; it is the abuse of others for self-glorification or self-gratification; it is the way of fallen humanity that would lord it over others if only they could. Three systematic theologians, Richard Roberts (chapter 9), Alan Torrance (chapter 6), and Lawrence Osborn (chapter 10) in their very different papers in this collection present a thoroughly theological critique of the abuse of power and the misuse of authority.

The second advantageous feature of the abusive model is that it forces us to look at denominational Christianity rather than seeing harmful religion as the exclusive property of fundamentalist religion or cults. Cultic behaviour can occur in the heart of the mainline churches too. This seems to hold true for Opus Dei in the Catholic Church, and for a short time in the life of the Nine O'Clock Service in Sheffield. Indeed, in my opinion, in many a church and chapel, as well as the cult and the coven, widespread and occasionally systematic abuse occurs that we can properly call 'harmful religion'.

Such widespread abuse can of course be deliberately orchestrated by unscrupulous persons, those whom George Tarleton, former 'apostle' in the house church movement, once called 'wrong 'uns'.[10] It is likely, however, that such abuse is rare; more typically it results from well-meaning, misguided or deluded authority figures (see Dave Tomlinson, chapter 2, and Russ Parker, chapter 4); or simply through the unreflective practice of sedimented traditions and conventional wisdom (see Sarah Boss, chapter 7). Endemic religious harm, such as incipient racism, or sexual discrimination, can exist through institutional practices which are so long-standing as to seem hallowed by time.

Systematic religious abuse, on the other hand, will more typically occur in tightly-knit structures that lend themselves to manipulation and authoritarian control rather than in looser structures where authority is diffuse, or where it is clearly delineated in a sensible, rational, yet personal way. This is particularly apposite for the psychological abuse more usually associated with the cults and the more extreme sects (see Dave

Tomlinson, chapter 2, and Steve Hunt, chapter 3). Geographical and/or socially isolated communities under the tutelage of an authoritarian leader would be paradigm candidates for potential abuse, but we must realize that if this holds true for cults and exclusivist sects, it also holds for monasteries and covenanted communities. The line between saints and fanatics is thin. This sadly is the message of Julius Rubin's chapter on an Anabaptist community, 'The Other Side of Joy', in chapter 5.

We should recognize also that mainline churches can suffer from what we might call 'sectarian implants'. In-crowds or ginger groups that are secretive, and hence not openly accountable, are breeding grounds for abuse. This seems to fit the story of the Nine O'Clock Service, and there have been complaints about charismatic groups which have moved in and taken over Anglican and Baptist churches.[11] The sectarian implant becomes 'the church within the church' which hatches elitist mentalities and delusional qualities, authoritarian controls and ideologies of power. Ginger groups can of course pep people up, but they can also force people out.

This leads to the third recommended feature of the abusive model of harmful religion. By concentrating more on the formal institutional structures and its officers and less on individual members of lay congregations, we encourage the moral virtues of stewardship, responsibility and accountable leadership. Furthermore, the model looks to the spiritual fruits of repentance and restitution, which may be more true to the gospel than therapeutic and counselling methodologies for combating addiction.

Nevertheless, the abusive model has its own dangers. First, when applying it to others, especially those in authority, it is important not only to get our facts right but also not to flaunt a judgmentalism that in reality hides our own wrongdoing. Motes in other people's eyes always seem bigger to us because of the beams in our own (Matthew 7:3). Sometimes our judgments are little more than sour grapes at other people's successes. New Church leader, Terry Virgo,[12] has made the observation that 'where there is life there are accidents', and while this might be viewed as a legitimation for mistakes, it is a reasonable observation that lively, enthusiastic churches are more likely to exhibit difficulties than ones which are barely alive.

The second danger with the abusive model is the possibility that we will let our genuine concern to protect others from harm interfere with legitimate religious freedom. Martin Reardon deals with this issue magisterially in chapter 1. Harmful religion is a religious belief or practice which damages or hurts somebody spiritually, mentally or physically. It is not religion that is not to our taste, or which we think may be mistaken in its beliefs. To apply the Christian concept of heresy to other world faiths is illegitimate. Muslims view Christians as 'infidels', outsiders in relation to true religion, and not heretics. As Lawrence Osborn observes, Christians have applied a similar distinction between insiders and outsiders, but have not in the past been averse to calling Jews and Muslims heretics.

Much reflection and discernment is needed clearly to distinguish harmfulness per se from community practices that may strike the outsider as inflicting pain of some kind, but which are considered normative by members. Physical abuse in religion, for example, could be said to cover the spectrum of harm from immolation to mutilation (including female 'circumcision' and emasculation), torture to male circumcision, and even from tattooing to corporal punishment and the deprivation of food and sleep. Many Christian traditions encourage fasting. North African Christians tattoo their bodies. Jews, Arabs and many Christians, too, circumcize their boys.

Christians will not condone or ignore immolation, emasculation, mutilation, torture, and female 'circumcision', but they will be divided over the other examples given above (although the *castrato* did not disappear from Vatican choirs until the twentieth century). We can see, at the very least, that religious physical abuse will range from strong to weak, high to low levels, the horrific to the painful, the unacceptable to the tolerable. In some cases, we may want to say that the language of harmfulness is inappropriate. Examples of this might include the voluntary ascetic endeavours of monks in numerous world faiths, not to mention initiation rites in many tribal cultures which do not fall under the unacceptable practices of emasculation or mutilation.

The definition and scope of harmful religion

The chapters in this book raise many questions about harmful religion which are inevitably controversial and unresolved. Dave Tomlinson, for example, sees authoritarian and conservative groups as having a built-in propensity to abuse. Alan Torrance's reflections on 'political correctness', however, demonstrate that abuse is neither the exclusive property of the right wing nor of conservatism. Perhaps conservatism, like liberalism, can also provide models of openness, fair play and decency.

Certainly it is too easy, if we are not careful, to forget that what might appear to be extremism or heavy-handedness in new churches might also be a natural function of the early phases of a religious organization in the full flush of joy. It is doubtful if we would approve today of John Wesley's autocratic control of early Methodism, or the severity with which the early Church dealt with wayward catechumens. And even benign charismatic leaders, such as General Booth of the Salvation Army in the 1860s, or Principal George Jeffreys of the Elim movement in the 1920s, found it difficult to relinquish control to more democratic forces.

Even if we wanted to retain our reservations about 'shepherding' (see chapter 2) and the abuse of healing and exorcist practices (chapters 3 and 4), it is surely important not to pay undue attention to the new and relatively small churches at the expense of looking more objectively at the far older and larger churches.[13] In this respect, Richard Roberts (chapter 9) raises important questions about the Turnbull report of the Church of England, because he wonders whether what appears to be a progressive agenda may in fact smuggle into religion all the managerial techniques of secular organizations which could militate against legitimate pastoral and spiritual concerns.

By the same token, David Martin (chapter 8) wonders whether the seemingly Christian concern to accept collective and national guilt is not a harmful distortion of the Christian doctrine of redemption.[14] If Martin's target is a certain liberal religiosity – now so deep in the heart of the mainstream churches – Sarah Boss, as a committed Roman Catholic (chapter 7) dares to ask whether there are not images of the *Theotokos* and other women saints that have not harmed women. Her carefully argued paper also turns this argument on its head by demonstrating that images of the Virgin Mother have been beneficial both to men and women.

Sociologist Steve Hunt's paper (chapter 3) is ostensibly a warning against some forms of exorcism, but it can also be read as a contribution from the anti-psychiatry lobby. Hunt is careful not to highlight harmful religion without also being aware that abuse can occur in the heart of the therapeutic professions. Other social scientists, like Foucault, for example, have argued that psychiatric ideology and methodology act in much the same way as religion and raise the very same issues of potential psychological abuse and the misuse of power.[15] Such a perspective, even if we think it jaundiced, should at least alert us to the fact that harm and abuse are a potential feature of all human relationships and not only religious ones.

The fact that this book, on the whole, has leaned towards an abusive rather than an addictive model of harmful religion will appeal to those who are strongly committed to justice and reparation for damage caused to others. For other practitioners involved in healing and holistic approaches to psychological abuse, the addictive model of religious abuse may have greater appeal. There is a danger, after all, that personal responsibility for religious addiction can be projected onto other actors so that indiscriminate accusations can be made against innocent parties. The delicate yet controversial area of repressed or lost memory syndrome in the field of sexual abuse is witness to the caution that needs to be used. For Christians, both the abusive and addictive models are complementary rather than contradictory or competitive. In the

New Testament, we read that Jesus healed the sick and bound up the broken-hearted, but he also condemned the oppressive and abusive religious leaders of his day.

As for us, we are told by our Lord in terms of uncompromising severity what will happen to us if we harm the weak, the innocent, and especially the children: 'But whoso shall offend one of these little ones which believe in me, it were better for him that a millstone were hanged about his neck, and that he were drowned in the depth of the sea. Woe unto the world because of offences! for it must needs be that offences come; but woe to that man by whom the offence cometh!' (Matthew 18:6-7).

Religious Abuse

Freedom, Authority and Power from a
Christian Perspective
Martin Reardon

━━━━━━━━━━

Cicero and Lactantius did not agree about the root of the Latin word *religio*. Did it come from the verb *religare*, meaning 'to bind', as Lactantius and later St Augustine thought? Or did it come from the verb *relegere*, meaning 'to go over and over again', as Cicero believed? Today, this debate might be of little more than etymological interest, were it not for the fact that from Roman times until today the word 'religion' has been very imprecise. In Latin, the word *religio* was used both for the inner, pure reality of reverence for God, and the outward trappings of rites and ceremonies.

Clearly, the nature of religion is of fundamental concern for our subject. It is difficult to show that we are abusing something unless we know what it is. I remember a few years ago being visited by a guru of a new religious movement and one of her disciples. She invited me to visit her religious centre. It was, she said, in a beautiful country house in a peaceful setting with a large garden. The religious community who lived there were very friendly and would welcome me to an old-fashioned English afternoon tea. 'What could be closer to the heart of true religion?' she asked. I looked up quickly into her face and the face of her spellbound disciple who was sitting on the floor, assuming that she was making a joke. But she was entirely serious.

Until then I had considered the major abuses of religion to be such things as coercion, using immoral means of persuasion, attracting very young people without the knowledge of their parents, etc. After she left, however, I began to think that it might be a greater abuse of religion to trivialize it. Afternoon tea in an English country garden among hospitable company is undoubtedly very pleasant, but is it religion?

What is religion?

So what do I, as a Christian in what I regard as the orthodox tradition (with a small 'o'), believe religion is? I believe it is a binding and permanent reverence for and relationship to a God who is both transcendent and immanent. Because God transcends the world, the only way to live is to be dependent, to make God the centre and meaning of life. Because God came into the world in Jesus Christ and is immanent in the Holy Spirit, Christians are called upon to respond in the power of the Spirit by living a life that will, so far as possible, reflect the self-sacrificing character of God as revealed in human form in Jesus Christ.

I recognize that there are other religions in the world which focus on other figures in the past or present, or exclusively on the immanence of God. Some of these I respect deeply, and I am prepared to learn from them, but they are not the Christian religion. If, as I believe, the Christian religion transcends the self in general and myself in particular, in its deepest sense it judges me. At its heart I do not judge it. Therefore I have a problem with the very concept of the use and abuse of religion. I use my reason in the *interpretation* of the Christian religion; but insofar as religion is revealed by God, it is what creates my standard of right and wrong, of use and abuse, and is not for me to judge.

That is not to say, of course, that the way religious people practise their religion is beyond criticism. The Protestant Reformers said the Church was always subject to reform. Dietrich Bonhoeffer went even further by talking of 'religionless Christianity'. In this way he distinguished the revelation of Christ and his immediate challenge of right and wrong, from the merely human interpretation and its attendant trappings, which are described as 'religion'. The Roman Catholic, Yves Congar, made a somewhat similar distinction between the 'essential elements' of the Catholic faith, which were irreformable, and the 'state of affairs', or historical context and interpretation of the essentials which inevitably resulted when the church tried to apply the essentials in any particular historical circumstances. These were always subject to reform. The essentials were irreformable.

As a reformed Christian (with a small 'r') I am quite prepared to discuss with the followers of Bonhoeffer what is merely human and subject to abuse in religion, and what is divine revelation, which must be obeyed. As a catholic (with a small 'c') Christian I am quite prepared to discuss with the followers of Congar what is merely a state of affairs and subject to abuse, and what is essential to the catholic faith. As a Christian therefore I am prepared to distinguish that part of my religion which judges me and gives me my sense of right and wrong from that merely human part which is capable of abuse.

My problem is, by what criteria do I judge the religion of a Jew, a Muslim, a Hindu or a Buddhist – let alone that of a Scientologist, a Rajneeshi, or a member of the Unification Church? Do I judge them by Christian criteria, or are there some universal criteria by which I can define what is religious abuse?

In our modern pluralistic and individualistic society, this question looks very different from how it looked three or four hundred years ago in this country – let alone how it looked in the Roman Empire – or even how it looks today to the Orthodox Church in Russia, or to the Muslims in Sudan as they enforce the *Shari'a* Law.

In the Roman Empire, everyone had to worship the emperor. It was both treasonable and atheistic not to do so. Only one people was excused: the Jews. Although they refused to worship the emperor, since they believed in only one God, the God of Israel, the empire reckoned that they were not in fact a threat to the *imperium* of the emperor. Religion in the Roman Empire had become an aspect of the state. Not a lot of people believed in the divinity of the emperor, least of all some of the emperors. Thus there is the story of one emperor saying on his deathbed: 'I think I am becoming a god'. However, religion was part of the cement that held the empire together. As long as people worshipped the emperor, they could worship any other gods they liked. And so a distinction grew up between public religion and a whole host of private or mystery religions or cults, such as those of Mithras or Dionysius.

If Christians had been prepared to worship the emperor and to treat their Christianity as a private religion, they would not have been persecuted. It was because they shared with the Jews a belief in one God, and because some Roman emperors saw them spreading rapidly and therefore, unlike the Jews, as a threat to the empire, that they put the Christians to death. When the last of the pagan emperors, Julian the Apostate, saw that he was losing this struggle with the Christians, he is reputed to have said as he lay dying: 'You have conquered, Galilean!' And so, after nearly three centuries of Christianity, the Emperor Constantine himself became a Christian, and, some would say, Christianity became compromised by too close an association with state coercive power.

For several centuries, the Christian religion became, in a number of different ways, tied to the state, tribe or nation. When Paulinus came to the court of King Edwin of Northumbria, the king consulted his advisors and together they decided that Northumbria should change its religion. The peasants were not consulted. At the Reformation, the civil powers decided which brand of the Christian religion would be allowed in their area – *cuius regio, eius religio*. The power of religion to bind together or divide a nation was very well understood, and monarchs tried to unite their people with the help of religion. Queen Mary burned Protestants on the grounds of their being heretics. Queen Elizabeth I cannily executed Catholics on the grounds that they were treasonably supporting the Catholic enemies of her realm. The modern concept of the freedom of religion was born in this era among what are now called the Free Churches, and the Pilgrim Fathers fled to North America in search of religious freedom. It was several centuries before the Acts of Uniformity of Reformation England were repealed, and freedom of religion was accepted in England. In 1948, the United Nations published the Universal Declaration of Human Rights, which includes the following:

> Everyone has the right to freedom of thought, conscience and religion: this right includes freedom to change his religion or belief, and freedom, either alone or in the community with others and in public or private, to manifest his religion or belief in teaching, practice, worship and observance.

The triumph of religious freedom in England has been followed by a widespread belief that religion is a private affair. Lord Melbourne is reputed to have said that 'things have come to a pretty pass when religion is allowed to invade public life'. However, society is not sure whether religion is a purely private affair. Religion in England is still thought of as beneficial to society as a whole. That is why it still has charitable status.

The government document, *Charities: A Framework for the Future*,[1] traces charitable status to the Charitable Uses Act of 1601:

> Guidance on what was to be considered charitable was found there in a list of objects which included:
> Relief of aged impotent and poor people... the maintenance of sick and maimed soldiers and mariners, schools of learning, free schools and scholars in universities... the repair of bridges, ports, havens, causeways, churches... and others.

Much of this work before the Reformation, and some of it afterwards, was being done by the churches and religious communities. So it was not surprising that religion itself – at that stage, of course, the Christian religion – was regarded as charitable. Indeed, the very concept of 'charity' is a Christian concept.

For all practical purposes, the courts have, for many years, accepted the classification which was made by Lord Macnaghten in 1891 in what has now become well known as the 'Pemsel' case.

This classification (which does not constitute a definition) reads as follows:

> Charity in its legal sense comprises four principle divisions – trusts for the relief of poverty, trusts for the advancement of education, trusts for the advancement of religion, and trusts for other purposes beneficial to the community, not falling under any of the previous heads.

With the growth in religious toleration, and with the development of a multi-cultural society in the United Kingdom, the courts have progressively admitted to charitable status a variety of Christian and other religious faiths. Gifts to dissenting Protestant churches and for the advancement of the Jewish and Roman Catholic faiths have been upheld by the courts as being of charitable purpose. The Commissioners have also registered trusts for the advancement of the Hindu, Sikh, Islamic and Buddhist religions.

The present position is that any religious body is entitled to charitable status so long as its tenets are not morally subversive and so long as its purposes are directed to the benefit of the public. The modern attitude of the courts is summed up in the often quoted remark of Mr Justice Cross, later Lord Cross of Chelsea: 'As between religions, the law stands neutral, but it assumes that any religion is at least likely to be better than none.' More recently, in the Australian Scientology Case, A.C.J. Mason and J. Brennan of the High Court of Australia held that: 'There can be no acceptable discrimination between institutions which take their character from religions which the majority of the community recognizes as religious and institutions which take their character from religions which lack that general recognition'. These dicta are important in drawing attention to the understandable reluctance of the courts to judge the relative worth of different religions or the truth of competing religious doctrines, all of which may have a place in a tolerant and culturally diverse society.

The government document from which I have been quoting was consultative. I am out of touch with any later developments, but the thrust of government thinking in 1989 was neither to change the law, nor to discriminate between one religious movement and another on religious grounds. Instead, they made it clear that the Charity Commissioners already had the power to remove from the Charity register any religious movement whose conduct was judged to have caused harm, and therefore not to be for the public benefit.

I will return to the issue of the conduct of religions and whether they are for the public benefit later. I include the reference to charitable status here because it shows that, although religious affiliation is now thought of as a private affair, religion is still understood as being of public importance and concern and largely beneficial. Though the privatization of religion in North America has gone much further than in England, the public attitude there is similar as regards its social importance and benefit. I am told that there used to be posters on the streets urging people 'to serve their community by attending the church of their choice'.

Religious freedom

When religion was a group, tribal or national affair, individuals who wished to practice a religion different from others had to do so very privately, or to emigrate, as the Pilgrim Fathers did. As we have seen, it took centuries for religious liberty to be recognized in England. For the Roman Catholic Church, the problem was even greater.

The post-Constantinian Christian Church has not had a clean record on religious abuse. Far from it. The Crusaders who tried to recapture the Holy Land by force from the Muslims; the Crusaders who turned aside to destroy their Orthodox co-religionists in Constantinople as an easier target than the Muslims; the Inquisition; the persecution of dissenters before and during the Reformation, particularly by Roman Catholic and Anglican countries, are all a stain on the name of Christ. It is significant that some of those now regarded as saints refused in their day to participate in such abuse. St Francis went unarmed across the Crusader lines to talk with their Muslim enemies about peace, and was courteously and generously received, but to no avail.

It was not until the Second Vatican Council in 1962 that the Roman Catholic Church argued itself out of a theology and practice on religious freedom which had until then been ambiguous. There had been tendencies among Roman Catholics to apply a double standard – freedom for the Church when it was in a minority; intolerance of others when it was in a majority. Pope Pius XII had rejected religious freedom as late as 1953 in his *Allocution on Tolerance*, basing his argument on the traditional opinion that truth had rights, but error had none. The Decree on Religious Liberty was the most controversial decree in the Second Vatican Council, because it raised the whole question of the apparent conflict between truth and freedom of belief. When the decree was promulgated at the end of 1965, Pope Paul VI called it one of the major texts of the council. It owed a lot to the thinking of such theologians as Congar and Newman. In fact, Newman had stated the decree's position neatly a century earlier in a famous toast: 'If I am obliged to bring religion into after-dinner toasts (which doesn't seem quite the thing), I shall drink to the Pope, if you please – still to Conscience first, and to the Pope afterwards.'[2]

Religious freedom is now formally accepted by all the Christian churches – although rather late in the day by some churches, including the Church of England and the Roman Catholic Church – or is it? After the destruction of the Iron Curtain, the Russian Orthodox Church, I understand, has been trying to exclude certain evangelical churches and new religious movements from what it regards as its own territory – Mother Russia. Before we cast metaphorical stones, let us recognize how difficult the application of religious freedom is in practice. Small religious groups entered the new Russia, which had no sophisticated method of limiting immigration, as Western European countries have. These groups came with much desired American dollars. Some of them unscrupulously dangled them before would-be converts, and, if the Russian Orthodox authorities are right, were as ready to make converts from Orthodoxy as from atheists. I pass no judgment here. I cite this example merely to show that although the Christian churches have accepted the principles of religious liberty, applying them is not always simple, especially in a society less accustomed to individualism than our own, and in desperate need of maintaining community and coherence in the face of threats of disintegration.

Authority and power

I now pass to what I consider the key issue, that of authority and power. It has been an axiom of most recent Free Church thought on the nature of the Church that Christian authority must be purely moral and spiritual. True authority, it is claimed, is personal. Its aim is to transform personality with the full will of the person to be transformed.

In his book, *The Authority of Jesus*, Dr Lee-Woolf recognizes the paradox that in Christ the Christian achieves full, personal freedom and yet still experiences Christ's authority. Few Christians would quarrel with this. The Russian Orthodox writer Khomiakhov states that the light of faith, like the impulse of love, must be the true internal and above all liberating authority, for the living member of the Church. It releases the Christian from all (external) authority and proclaims not only the right but also the duty of freedom.[3] On the other hand, of course, in any human society there must be external authority if order is to be maintained.

These two standpoints are by no means mutually exclusive. Authority must begin by being external, as Lee-Woolf states. The ultimate, most effective and transforming authority, however, will be that which obtains not merely external but free, internal and intelligent obedience. By this means the command of external authority becomes the desire of the will.

Authority is external and its aim is the transformation of

persons. Can we then use force to support authority? What is the essential nature of authority within the Church, and what is its relationship to the actual exercise of corporate ecclesiastical power? First we must notice that force can be exerted in a great number of different ways. There is an infinite number of gradations, where physical, psychological, moral and spiritual forces are mixed. In this world do not all authoritative decisions in practice carry more than purely moral and spiritual force?

As soon as a Church exists which accepts some pastoral responsibility for its members, it exercises authority. The model for the Church is Christ himself. Christ and his disciples had to exercise pastoral responsibilities. It was Christ's responsibility to choose his disciples, to teach and guide them. This responsibility he handed on, in some measure, to his apostles in the duty of pastoral care and the power of the keys. It has to be exercised continually in the Church.

Often the exercise of this responsibility may seem like a final judgment. But properly understood, it is merely the pronouncement of general divine truth, and its application by fallible human beings to particular cases.

This is so because we live in the times between the coming of Christ on earth in Palestine and the final judgment. The twelve disciples were given an office in the New Testament (Matthew 19:28; Revelation 21:14). This office carried an absolute and final authority – the authority of a judge – the very authority that God the Father had invested in his Son. Yet, like Christ's authority, it was not to be fully and finally exercised till the end of the age. The authority that the disciples are to exercise in this world is that of the servant and pastor, which is the same as Christ exercised in his earthly ministry (Luke 22:24-32; John 21:15-17). In the life of Christ, these two functions are found together pre-eminently in his humble submission – in the feet-washing, Gethsemane and Golgotha. And one may see the same ministry prophesied for St Peter in John 21:18 and realized for St Paul in his sufferings for the 'care of all the churches' (2 Corinthians 11:28).

21

Jesus did not seek to be worshipped, though the woman with the jar of ointment was not rejected. Jesus even seemed to avoid making practical judgments, such as the elders of a synagogue would have to make, for example in the case of the woman taken in adultery. Yet in one circumstance at least, Jesus was prepared to use at least a show of force, or at least to accept the psychological support of popularity with the crowds, as when he overthrew the tables of the moneychangers in the Temple (John 2:15; Matthew 21:12; Mark 11:15). In my view, this act was in the nature of a sign or symbolic action in the tradition of the Old Testament prophets, rather than a serious attempt to clear the temple by force. Certainly, the Second Vatican Council's Decree on Religious Liberty is in tune with all other contemporary church statements in utterly repudiating all coercion in religion. In practice, however, it has to be admitted that the boundary between coercion and persuasion is often blurred, and constant vigilance is required to see that the boundary is preserved.

How in practice is this boundary to be preserved? In 1986, the Executive Committee of the British Council of Churches asked the Board for Mission and Unity of the Church of England to prepare some pastoral guidelines in relation to New Religious Movements. In trying to produce guidelines for this purpose, I was pleasantly surprised that some Church institutions had already produced guidelines for their own purposes to ensure that their members kept within the boundary of religious freedom. Some of those guidelines were used in producing the following *Draft Code of Practice*:

In view of the current controversies over the behaviour of some New Religious Movements, the Board puts forward, as a draft for discussion, the following Code of Practice which all religions, new and old, should adhere to, including our own:

The Board deplores:

(a) Inviting people to an event under false pretences, without explaining the true nature and purpose of the event;

(b) Raising money under false pretences, or not making clear the purposes for which the money will be used and the name and nature of the organization for which it is being collected;

(c) Hiding the true identity of persons trying to raise money or to attract others into their movement;

(d) Using unfair or immoral means of persuasion such as 'heavenly deception', 'flirty fishing', sleep deprivation, food deprivation, hypnosis or any form of emotional, psychological or spiritual 'blackmail';

(e) Concealing from prospective adherents some of the implications and consequences of accepting membership of the movement before requiring commitment;

(f) Serious discussion with minors without the knowledge of parents, guardians or schoolteachers, and refusal or unreasonable hindering of access to adherents or prospective adherents;

(g) Offering financial gain as an inducement;

(h) Failure to be publicly accountable in the use of finance and resources where money has been raised from public sources;

(i) Irresponsibility in employment of students and staff, failing to pay national insurance contributions, refusing reasonable access to medical care, etc.

On the other hand the Board also deplores:

(a) All attempts at the forcible 'deprogramming' of adherents of New Religious Movements;

(b) All attempts to declare illegal or withdraw rights from a New Religious Movement without evidence, acceptable by a court of law, that it is acting illegally or has done so.

(c) Any lack of concern for the truth and spreading of misinformation.

(d) Any denial of the right of an individual freely to choose his or her religious beliefs.[4]

These draft guidelines were produced for a particular purpose in a particular situation. If they were to be used more widely, they would need to be broadened considerably. They made it clear, however, that any guidelines should apply to all religious bodies, including the mainline churches. The media have in recent times been full of accounts of religious abuse in the mainline churches. Such abuse is extremely serious and needs to be guarded against by constant vigilance. It is, I think, significant that this abuse has often occurred when a particular congregation or minister has been permitted a great deal of freedom to act without supervision. Proper structures of authority are required in order to maintain freedom and to prevent religious abuse in the churches. As we have seen from the example of Jesus Christ, true authority and the proper respect for freedom are not mutually antagonistic but necessary to one another, if freedom is not to slide into licence and authority into coercion.

There have been proposals to bring in special laws for religion in order to prevent religious abuse. For the reasons I gave at the beginning of this chapter, I believe these are impracticable and probably undesirable unless or until we have a much clearer and generally acceptable definition of religion. However, this should not worry us in the United Kingdom, since the existing general law of the land and the powers of the Charity Commissioners are such as to be able to act against religions whose tenets are morally subversive or whose conduct is a threat to the public good. Should the general law or the powers of the Charity Commissioners prove inadequate at any point, they could be amended.

What might be helpful is a code of practice drawn up by religious bodies themselves to guard against abuse. Other public bodies have had to produce such codes. Is it time for religious bodies to get together to produce one? It would not be easy, but it might help to guard against religious abuse.

The Inter-Faith Network for the United Kingdom has already produced a leaflet, agreed by representatives of many different religions, which provides guidelines on building good relationships between people of different faiths.[5] However, to produce an agreed code of practice to guard against religious abuse would take us back to the question with which I began – are we able to agree on what we mean by religion?

2

Shepherding: Care or Control?

Dave Tomlinson

'Shepherding' is a term that emerged in this country in the mid 1970s among the so-called house churches. Based on the New Testament metaphor of leaders as shepherds to the flock of God, shepherding claimed to be nothing more than a present-day interpretation of the sort of pastoral care that existed in the early Church. In many ways, its original aims and intentions were laudable and the practice flourished against a backdrop of contemporary Church culture where pastoral care frequently amounted to little more than the customary visitation of the elderly and the sick and a friendly exchange after the Sunday services.

However, while the intentions may have been admirable and while many people, even now, will readily testify to the help and support they gained through the practice of shepherding, stories also abound as to the harm and damage it caused. So what is the truth about shepherding? Was it simply a valid form of pastoral care that on occasions suffered from over-zealous implementation, or were there aspects of its practice that were inherently wrong and possibly dangerous? And, indeed, is it actually correct to refer to it as something purely in the past, or is shepherding still being practised whether under this or another name? Most important of all, what lessons can be learned from the shepherding experience?

Before tackling these questions I need to say a word or two about my own background and outline briefly my involvement in the 'shepherding' movement. Having grown up in the Plymouth Brethren, I became involved with an early charismatic group in Liverpool during the mid 1960s. This led to immense tension between myself and the Brethren elders, who finally offered me the choice of either renouncing my charismatic experience or leaving the church. Not surprisingly, I chose to leave and, thereafter, became deeply involved with the newly emerging house church movement, where I was soon acknowledged as a promising young leader.

During the early 1970s, along with my wife Pat, I pioneered my first independent house church in a small North Yorkshire town and in the years that followed I was instrumental in the planting of various other new churches. Before long, I developed an itinerant ministry within the house church movement and by 1975 I was recognized as an apostle not only by the churches I served but, more significantly, by the influential grouping of men already accepted as apostles. I am aware that to those outside the movement, the term 'apostle' sounds pretentious, possibly bizarre, but in practice the apostles are simply the bishops of the house church movement.

Dr Andrew Walker, whose book *Restoring the Kingdom* remains the most credible account of the development of the house church movement, plots its evolution around the memorable twin rubrics of R^1 and $R^2 - R^1$ signifying those churches characterized by a more robust authority structure and R^2 signifying those with a somewhat looser, less authoritarian framework.[1] The 'R' stands for 'restoration', an ideology that still characterizes most strands of the house church movement, that of restoring in today's world the original pattern of New Testament Christianity.

Up until the late 1970s, I functioned as an apostle in the R^1 camp, the one that most unequivocally adopted the language and practice of shepherding. By the end of that period, I led a team of fifteen people who gave oversight to some fifty or so house churches in different parts of the country. I will not pause at this stage to say how and why I decided to depart from the shepherding movement, as I shall touch on this a little later.

The practice of 'shepherding'

The house church movement evolved as a result of the conflict generated in the mainstream churches by the onset in the 1960s and 1970s of the so-called charismatic movement. Incidentally, in this context, 'charismatic' is being used in a theological rather than a sociological sense. It refers to the phenomenon in which people claim to experience a filling with the Holy Spirit as at Pentecost and, as a result, exercise *charismata* or the 'gifts of the Spirit' spoken of by the apostle Paul, gifts such as speaking in tongues, prophecy and healing. While this phenomenon has been commonplace throughout the twentieth century within Pentecostal churches, the charismatic movement signalled a distinct shift. Pentecostal phenomena such as speaking in tongues now began to take place within the mainstream denominations. In the considerable conflict that this generated and in the bitterness that ensued many of the charismatics either left or were asked to leave their churches.

This exodus from the mainstream churches did not lead, as one might have expected, to a great swelling of the ranks of the traditional Pentecostal churches. Instead, all across the country, hundreds of small new groups sprang up, meeting in people's front rooms. Liberated from their conflict with those who condemned the charismatic phenomenon and revelling in the freedom to explore it unhindered, these young 'house churches' flourished and increased in numbers week by week. Leadership in the groups was extremely laid back – everyone was delighted to shed the trappings of formal religion in favour of what was perceived to be a more Spirit-led approach to Church. There was no formal liturgy, no structure, no clergy to keep control; the Spirit could speak in any way through any person. These were heady days of glorious anarchy and many who lived through them still recall the period with great warmth and enthusiasm.

The freedom of this early period was difficult to sustain. Looking back on these times, George Tarleton, one of the then leaders of the house church movement (who has subsequently forsaken it altogether) recollects: 'We began to realize that we were riding an anarchic animal. Anything could happen... We could go anywhere, do anything.' While relishing this anarchy, Tarleton also recalls the sense of responsibility he and others felt to ensure that the 'God-given chaos' did not descend into some kind of disaster.[2] It also became clear that the experience of the Spirit was no cover-all solution for people's individual problems and that deeper pastoral needs could not be met through enthusiastic glossalalic intercessions and the laying on of hands. As time went by, the feeling grew that some kind of new structure was necessary; yet it needed to be a structure that was congruous with the charismatic character of what was going on.

It is useful to note the significant overlap between our present use of the term 'charismatic' and its more established sociological meaning. According to Max Weber, the sociologist who explored this field extensively, a charismatic movement is a phenomenon that occurs where an established institutional order either breaks down and becomes disorganized or simply runs out of steam and loses the ability to satisfy or represent people. The kind of leadership that then emerges will be based on personal charisma (theological or otherwise – or both) and upon a recognition of the exceptional or even supernatural qualities of individual 'charismatic' leaders. In contrast to traditional or bureaucratic authority structures, Weberian charismatic authority has no mechanisms for appointment or dismissal, no career structure and no training or qualifications – a very accurate description of the kind of leadership that emerged and, to a large degree, still exists among the house churches.[3] Naturally, such leadership frequently brings great benefits to its followers, yet it also carries considerable dangers.

However, to return to our story, it was the growing desire among house church people for a satisfactory balance between Spirit and structure that eventually opened the door to the practice of shepherding. Numerous influences contributed. For example, there were the teachings of Watchman Nee, a greatly admired leader in China prior to the cultural revolution, whose books were widely read in the 1960s. Essentially a man of an earlier era, Nee was also a restorationist, as is clear from his book, *The Normal Christian Church Life*, in which he attempts to extract from the New Testament a normative pattern of Church structure based around an ongoing ministry of apostles and prophets.[4] Yet, far from being anarchic, Nee envisages the Church as a 'top down' structure of delegated authorities, in which everyone must be submissive and obedient to those above them. Indeed, he appears to advocate obedience to authority even against one's own better judgment: 'Whether the one in authority is right or wrong does not concern us since he has to be responsible directly to God. The obedient needs only to obey; the Lord will not hold us responsible for any mistaken obedience.'[5]

Outrageous though this undoubtedly is, it succeeded in entering the mind-set of many house church people, not least because of the distinction Nee drew between official or bureaucratic authority (that which arises out of human appointment) and what he called 'spiritual' authority (that which arises out of divine appointment or a divine 'anointing') – a distinction that appealed to many charismatics.

Although Watchman Nee provided a background influence in the shift from charismatic anarchy to charismatic authority, the real movement in this direction came with a visit to Britain in 1972 from a group of Argentinian pastors who addressed an enthusiastic audience of house church leaders on the subject of discipleship. 'Jesus didn't commission us to go and make converts,' they told us, 'but to make disciples'. From this premise, they went on to explain how authentic Christian ministry is not about the impartation of information but about the formation of people's lives. 'It's simple,' one of them explained. 'All you have to do is get your people committed and submitted and then you can get on with the real business of discipleship.'

In his best-selling little book, *Disciple*, Juan Carlos Ortiz, the most well known of the Buenos Aires pastors, testifies to the success of discipleship in his own church where, over a short period of time, his 1500 strong congregation was transformed from 'mere Church members' into a living network of disciples and disciplers. Like his colleagues who came to Britain, Ortiz emphasizes submission as the key to the process: 'If we are going to be people of authority,' he

30

states, 'we must all stand under authority for, only when I am in line, can authority pass through me to others.'[6]

During the period 1972-74, the themes of discipleship and spiritual authority spread rapidly throughout the house churches. Many of the groups, until then autonomous, began to get 'related' (a euphemism for submitted) to one of the apostles who were emerging ever more strongly and who were recognized as authorities appointed by God. Only when leaders were 'submitted to God's authority' themselves could they expect their people to be submitted to them.

This brings us to the third influence, the one that really established the notion of shepherding among the British house churches. The source was a small group of highly respected charismatic leaders in America known at the time as the 'Fort Lauderdale men'. The apparently remarkable feature of these men – Bob Mumford, Ern Baxter, Derek Prince, Charles Simpson and Don Basham – was the renunciation of their renowned individualism in favour of a 'covenant relationship' of mutual submission. Each of them represented a whole tribe of travelling preachers and local church leaders structured in a one-to-one pastoral system which they called 'shepherding'.

From 1974 to 1977, Ern Baxter, the senior statesman of the group, made numerous strategic visits to Britain, where his spellbinding oratory at events like the Dales and Capel Bible Weeks convinced literally thousands of people of the necessity to submit their lives to 'divinely appointed' shepherds. Baxter's apocalyptic portrayal of the end-time struggle between God's kingdom and the domain of darkness was graphic, and the only safe place to be in such days, he assured us, was under the 'covering' (another euphemism for submission) of God's shepherds. It is interesting to note how a strong apocalyptic vision frequently becomes an effective tool for the control of groups of religious people, and this was certainly the case with Baxter. Under the impact of his powerful rhetoric and persuasive, if dubious, teachings from the Bible, thousands of people left their traditional churches to place themselves under the care and covering of churches that embraced the notion and practice of shepherding.

It was, in fact, this combination of inspirational, charismatic preaching of the likes of Baxter and Mumford, along with the ready-made option of joining one of the flourishing networks of the home-grown apostles, that really placed the house churches on the ecclesiastical map in Britain during the mid 1970s.

The actual practice of shepherding

It may be helpful at this stage to outline how shepherding actually worked. Few churches in this country developed the intensely pyramidic structure advocated by the Argentinians and Americans. Here, the system evolved around three basic layers of leadership: home-group leadership, local church eldership, and apostolic team. Everyone who was an accepted member of a shepherding or restoration church had to belong to a home-group and this invariably demanded a pledge of commitment to the church and its leaders. Sometimes this was achieved simply through a verbal agreement to the particular church's membership criteria. In other cases, it involved actually signing a pledge of commitment and, on occasions, it even required one or more interviews with the elders. They decided whether or not the individual was truly ready and willing for commitment – some churches were notoriously difficult to join.

An essential element of commitment was a willingness to submit to the elders or their delegates – usually the home-group leaders – as well as to the apostolic team covering the church. In practice, this meant being prepared to receive input into one's personal life, into matters of character development, personal relationships, financial affairs or into any aspect of life thought to be necessary or appropriate. It also meant not going ahead with any important decisions without first submitting them to one's leaders. In many instances, submission to the leaders resulted in a virtual directive to move home. There are many cases where whole groups were required to up their roots and move to another area, according to the wisdom and strategic planning of the apostle. Stories even went around, some years ago, of a church in which members were expected to entrust the key to their front door to their shepherd. Personally, I never believed these reports, but only recently I talked with a couple who assured me that it did actually happen in their church – an R² church at that! However, on the whole, the practice of shepherding was not so intrusive and dictatorial as it may at first sound, and many people benefited from the help, advice and support they received.

As I have already indicated, the elders of a particular church were not the final layer of authority in the shepherding structure. They in turn were to be submitted to an apostle or the members of an apostolic team. Apostles were sometimes referred to as the 'shepherds to the shepherds', and it was expected that local church elders would receive regular input concerning their personal lives as well as the life of the church. Apostles were not, however, intended to be mini-popes, the theory being that they were submitted and accountable to one another. This was certainly the way that the whole package was sold at events like the Dales Bible Week, where people were encouraged to survey the men on the platform – and they were all men! These were men, it was said, who submitted their lives to one another and who functioned as a self-regulating collegiate. You were safe in their care.

I should also mention at this point the practice of tithing – giving one tenth of one's income – which was frequently tied to the system of shepherding. In his little book, *Discipleship, Shepherding, Commitment*, Derek Prince, one of the Fort Lauderdale men, argues for a New Testament principle that a shepherd is entitled to the financial support of his sheep. He also contends that just as money and possessions were entrusted to the apostles at Pentecost, so Church leaders should be similarly entrusted with them today.[7] As a result of this type of teaching, tithing was almost universally adopted among the house churches, as it still is today. In addition, it became commonplace that churches would 'tithe their tithes' to the apostle who was the shepherd to the church. As might be expected, some churches were much more diligent than others in ensuring that individuals paid their tithes but it was the high level of compliance that virtually guaranteed the sound financial basis of the house church movement.

Of course, this practice has not been without its critics and many former members of house churches complain about the pressure to tithe and, in some cases, of the expectation that individuals should give much more than a tithe. Most churches certainly included tithing as a condition of commitment to the church, and those people who objected that they could not really afford to tithe were generally told that they could not afford not to tithe. After all, how can God help you out of your financial difficulties if you do not start by accepting the divine principles of financial management!

Despite the attempts to ensure effective safeguards where shepherding was concerned, and, regardless of the benefits many people derived from its practice, lots of others speak of being hurt and abused by it. Indeed, over the past few years I have encountered hundreds of casualties and I suspect that this is the tip of an iceberg. Sometimes pain and suffering has been inflicted through the sheer naivety of a shepherd or through their incompetence to deal effectively with the issues in question. I think of Penny, for example, who struggled with bulimia but was encouraged to believe that her real problem was 'spiritual'.[8] Various methods were adopted to help Penny, including deliverance from a spirit of eating disorder and enforced eating plans. Of course, none of this worked, and her personal problems increased as she was made to feel that in some way she was to blame for the lack of progress.

Perhaps one of the greatest cruelties to Penny lay in her being forbidden to play a musical instrument in the worship group of the church on the basis that she 'had a problem' and would be unable, therefore, to 'play in the Spirit'. By denying her this and by failing simply to embrace her as a normal friend, the leaders of this group withheld the one thing they could have offered her – a sense of worth and self-esteem. Incidentally, this example is relatively recent and occurred in a church that would probably deny all connections with shepherding, even though it clearly does operate within that framework.

Sadly, this is no isolated case. I know of many people who have been ill-advised on financial decisions or who have been given poor counsel about their personal relationships, and have ended up experiencing great stress emotionally and relationally. I know people who have been led to believe that they were healed of some sickness and encouraged to cease taking medication, only to find themselves with much greater health problems, or being gripped by guilt because they were not healed – or both!

The problems created by shepherding were multiplied by the narrow-minded attitudes that undergirded its use. This has been especially the case with regard to marital and family relationships. Sonia and Tom, for example, lost their marriage through the imposition on their relationship of a sexist outlook. Sonia was a talented person who worked in the City and was well accustomed to holding her own in a male-dominated work environment. Naturally, she was no pushover in her relationship with Tom and, on occasions, she also spoke her mind to the church leaders. One day, Tom was taken aside by his shepherd and told that the elders viewed him as 'good leadership material'. However, there was a problem: he had to bring his wife into 'proper submission' if he wished to advance in the church. Like a fool, he attempted to follow this advice and his relationship with Sonia took a predictable nose-dive. Two years of painful conflict ensued, during which time Sonia was variously told that she was rebellious, possessed of the 'spirit of Jezebel', and living in disobedience to scripture. Given the circumstances, it would have been a miracle if their marriage had survived!

The oppression of women has in fact been rife through the shepherding movement. I remember a distraught young woman approaching me after hearing me give what she obviously considered to be a feminist perspective on the church. 'I'm confused,' she said. 'I've recently been delivered of a "spirit of feminism" by my elders, but now I'm wondering if I was really OK all along.' Having, I hope, helped her to recover her 'spirit of feminism', I advised her to reconsider whether her church was the most helpful place to be.

On an even more serious level, there was Kay, who was asked by her elders why she was thirty-nine years old and still not married. After an uncomfortable and distinctly bizarre forty-minute conversation, they finally came to the point: was she a lesbian? Graciously, she replied that she was not. 'So you would get married if the Lord gave you a husband, then?' one of the men prompted. Discomforted by the entire line of reasoning, Kay cautiously replied, 'I suppose so.' 'Well would you mind if we prayed with you about the matter?' the elder continued. At this point, Kay had taken more than she could stomach and wisely excused herself both from the meeting and the church!

But it is not just women who have suffered under the abusive aspects of shepherding. I know of numerous men who have been similarly hurt – some of them former leaders of house churches. For example, Jim, who had spent ten years planting and establishing a new church, decided it might be a good thing to come under the covering of an apostle. After a year of being in this arrangement, it was suggested that he had 'greater potential' than his church could provide and that he should move to the 'apostolic base', where he would be groomed for a wider ministry. Having moved, the 'wider ministry' turned out to be a menial job in a publications business, and the church he had planted was taken over by a member of the apostolic team and developed into a useful resource for the team's work! Jim eventually left the job and the church, vowing never to get involved with anything like this again.

Then there is Brian, a musician and worship leader who is still regularly visiting his doctor and taking anti-depressants. He resisted the move towards commitment and shepherding in his church and finally departed feeling bullied by the leaders, who persistently told him that he was resisting the Spirit. He had been a founding member of the church and considered the other leaders his friends. Now he felt betrayed and misunderstood. He recently told me that could not envisage ever joining another church.

My own departure from the shepherding scene came around 1980, as a result of growing disquiet at what I considered to be the trend towards greater authoritarianism. The matter was brought to a head by the way one of the leading house church apostles 'sanctioned' a church consisting of several hundred people, because their elders would not accept the man he believed to be their rightful leader. The elders had serious difficulties in trusting this particular man and refused to submit, with the result that the church became off-limits to anyone in committed relationship to the apostle.

I felt unable to accede to this judgment and saw it as an example of the way authority was now being understood and practised. Since none of the other apostles in the group joined me in my dissent, I decided that the best thing was to resign from the group – a decision I have never regretted.

Learning from the shepherding experience

One leading evangelical recently commented that shepherding was an experiment that had now been abandoned – but surely the subject cannot be brushed aside so hastily. To begin with, the practice still persists in certain house church circles, despite the protest that theirs is not 'heavy' shepherding. There are also other churches who, while not adopting the shepherding model as such, have, nevertheless, incorporated significant elements of it into their pastoral and leadership practice. A tragic example of this is seen in the case of the Nine O'Clock Service in Sheffield where Chris Brain, the so-called 'rave' vicar who in the summer of 1995 admitted to a series of improper sexual relations with women members of his church, apparently modelled his manipulative style of leadership on principles gained from shepherding. However, the broader if less obvious concern evoked by the shepherding experience is that of the narrow line that exists between care and control in many areas of Christian ministry.

37

One area of contemporary ministry that merits particular mention is that of the charismatic movement. The reason for doing this is twofold. Firstly, the shepherding experience arose directly out of the charismatic movement; indeed, it is questionable whether a movement such as shepherding can emerge without some kind of charismatic dimension. It will have been noted in this regard that in a number of the instances of abuse through shepherding cited above, the actual damage was created by a combination of shepherding and aspects of charismatic ministry – specifically that of deliverance from spirits. Secondly, there are elements in the present charismatic ethos that make it inherently susceptible to a slippage from care to control. What are these elements?

To begin with, charismatic meetings tend to be particularly characterized by an emphasis on ministering to people's personal needs, or perceived personal needs. This in itself can create vulnerability and cultivate patterns of dependency. Furthermore, the style of such ministry – deliverance from spirits, mental, emotional and physical healing, prophecies, words of knowledge, and the so-called 'Toronto Blessing' – is of an extraordinary nature and lends itself to the emergence of 'experts' who consequently attain significant status and power. There also exists in most charismatic meetings a strong sense of certainty and positiveness in which it is very difficult to express doubt or to question what is taking place or being said. On occasions, there is also a degree of conscious, albeit well intentioned, manipulation.

An example of this is found in some of the churches associated with the Toronto Blessing, where instruction sheets were circulated among leaders on how to 'administer the blessing'. These gave advice such as: 'Get those who have been touched to testify and then pray for them again. This brings great faith to the people'; and: 'Whenever there are first-timers, inform them as to what they may expect.' Arguably, however, the most dangerously manipulative element which underlies all these other points – and which is not necessarily limited to the charismatics – is the belief that anyone can emphatically say, 'this is what God is saying', or 'this is what

God is doing'. Of course, the problem is that once such statements are qualified with 'I think that this is what God is saying', or, 'it could be that this is of God', they immediately lose much of their appeal. Yet without such a shift of emphasis, I cannot help but feel that shepherding will always be crouching at the door of the charismatics.

Yet it is not just in the hothouse atmosphere of charismatic meetings that the line between care and control proves difficult to delineate. Many parish priests and mainstream church pastors know how easy it is to slip from one side of the line to the other. One of the reasons for this and, indeed, one of the reasons for the popularity of strong leaders in all sections of the Church, is that we live in an age of great uncertainty. Many people are attracted to those who appear to bring a sense of something that is definite and absolute – or better still, 'prophetic direction'.

Gilles Kepel's stimulating book, *The Revenge of God*, explores this phenomenon in the context of the three Abrahamic religions, where the strongly resurgent elements all appear to be in the fundamentalist sectors. Yet this new wave of fundamentalists, according to Kepel, 'are not drawn mainly from "obscurantist" groups of the population such as the illiterate and aged country people', they are predominantly young, educated people from the mainstream of society. The common factor among them is a passionately felt complaint about the fragmentation of society and of 'the absence of an overarching ideal worthy of their allegiance.'[9]

Another possible reason for the tendency towards patterns of dependent behaviour among churchgoers lies in the conservative and conformist nature of so many churches and denominations. Churches, on the whole, are not places where independent thinking is fostered, or where self-criticism is invited. In his description of four stages of spiritual growth, the popular writer and psychoanalyst Scott Peck observes that most churchgoers remain at stage two, the stage of conformity and institutionalism, and seldom progress to the third stage of independent thinking and necessary scepticism.[10] I have explored Peck's assertion further in my book, *The Post-Evangelical*, and suggested that part of the problem lies in the parental and paternalistic model upon which much Church leadership is based.[11]

Prevention is better than cure

Thankfully, abusive control of people such as was experienced in aspects of the shepherding movement or at the Nine O'Clock Service in Sheffield is relatively rare in churches. Yet an obligation rests on churches and Church leaders to ensure that patterns of control and dependency, no matter how apparently innocuous, are countered at every turn. I would suggest the following to be fundamental in this regard.

1. That churches maintain a strong participative style of ordering their affairs. Without wishing to plunge into intractable arguments about Church government, I would simply suggest that we need to move away from hierarchical expressions of Church leadership and explore structures that encourage maximum participation from Church members. People who are treated as adults and whose individual points of view are respected are much less likely to succumb to manipulative forms of control.

2. That Church leadership develops greater skills in facilitating and enabling. As we approach the millennium it is surely time to rethink the skills and training that are required for Church leadership. A bishop commented recently that, far from being prepared for the twenty-first century, much of the Church is still rooted in the nineteenth century.

It is no longer acceptable for ministers simply to take refuge in the pulpit – six feet above contradiction. We need leaders trained in the art of group facilitation, leaders committed to participative and experiential forms of learning, leaders capable of countering patterns of dependency and skilled at empowering people to take personal responsibility. Much can be gained in this regard from other fields; for example, from models being developed in industry, education and youth work.

3. That the development of critical faculties be seen as entirely compatible with growth in faith. We must set aside any notion of the incompatibility of faith and questioning and foster a more dialectical approach that can embrace both. All too often, Church leaders measure their own success by the degree of agreement they solicit from their congregations. Perhaps we should turn this on its head and judge our effectiveness by the degree to which people question what they hear – even from their own leaders. How about fostering an atmosphere in Church services so that people freely raise their hands to ask questions during sermons or talks? Or what about the idea of churches establishing their own debating societies? In an age of disillusionment with the quality of political debate, it would be gratifying to see the Church once again leading the way in promoting vigorous and constructive debate.

4. That Church leaders find the space to meet from time to time with a spiritual director – not a shepherd – who can help them reassess their own motivation and regularly cleanse themselves of the seductive will to control. No structure or system of accountability can ensure that things will not go wrong. There is no way around final responsibility resting on the personal integrity of individual leaders. In an ancient episode of the American TV soap, *Dallas*, J.R. Ewing was asked how he could perpetually abuse and manipulate people in the way he did. 'Oh it's easy,' J.R. replied. 'You just ditch integrity – the rest's a piece of cake!'

The shepherding era has, I suspect, something to teach us all. In practice, the line between care and control, between service and exploitation, is extremely thin and the time to start worrying is when we have convinced ourselves that we are safely ensconced on the right side of that line. We must evolve patterns of Church life that minimize the potential for manipulation and which foster a healthy level of critical independence on the part of Church members. Moreover, those of us in positions of leadership must never tire of searching our own hearts and motives. Like it or not – in some form or other – shepherding crouches at all our doors.

3

Giving the Devil More Than His Due

Some Problems with Deliverance Ministry

Steve Hunt

On one occasion, while sitting in the back of a car on the way to a charismatic church meeting, I listened intently to a story related by a woman who had recently left her fellowship. I knew there was something profoundly wrong, since she had not long joined and was a relative newcomer to the Christian faith. The problem was the deliverance ministry based at the church. This particular woman had undergone a kind of initiation ceremony, a veritable rite of passage meant to ensure that those joining the congregation were 'demon-free'.

Having being designated a candidate for deliverance, because of her West African cultural background, a team of some half a dozen people had arrived at her home to 'cleanse' it of 'demonic forces'. They proceeded to cast demons out of her fridge and demanded that she disposed of her toilet brush holder which was in the shape of a green frog and apparently attracted evil spirits. The lady saw this episode as typical of the way in which the 'deliverance team' were abusing their calling and holding considerable power over the congregation.

I have many other such accounts. There is, however, little to gain from merely relating a catalogue of horror stories, and there is as great a danger of being reduced to a paranoid hysteria concerning such practices as those who get carried away by them. Nevertheless, it is the misuse of deliverance which has, undoubtedly, caused untold harm in charismatic churches especially. Indeed, there are few other topics that have fuelled theological controversy and caused so much pastoral confusion in evangelical circles in the last few years.

To be sure, there is nothing particularly new in all this, since there exists documented and legendary instances of what might go wrong with deliverance and exorcism. One example was the infamous 'Barnsley case' in 1975,[1] when a man killed his wife after an all-night exorcism. Five years later, a mentally unstable woman died as a result of two apparently well-intentioned Christians attempting to rid her of the 'spirit of Judas Iscariot'.

Clearly, it is necessary to get things in perspective. There is something about conducting deliverance and exorcisms within the context of western society that is a particular anathema to the modern mind. Even when orthodox medical experts see virtues in the booming alternative therapies, a line is usually drawn at what they perceive as the more bizarre practice of putting evil spirits in their proper place. Moreover, it is easy to be unduly swayed by the self-appointed watchdogs of the media, who are more than capable of conducting their own witch-hunts for 'non-conformists', and it only takes a scent of an exorcism to launch them off on their own moral panics.

To be sure, exorcism of one form or another is a world-wide ritual that has existed for many centuries and remains an integral part of numerous cultural and religious belief systems. It is not primarily about persecution, superstition and ignorance, nor the abuse of power. From a cross-cultural perspective it performs a variety of functions, including overcoming emotional problems, precipitating emotional release, enhancing cathartic effects, re-establishing personal relationships, and bringing social solidarity for tribal and Third World peoples. Even in the charismatic Christian practice, there is good reason to suggest that deliverance may have some therapeutic qualities and that it can 'empower the patient' by helping a person to confront and overcome emotional difficulties if they themselves are convinced that they are associated with malevolent spiritual forces. These considerations, nevertheless, should not distract us from some of the very real and potential dangers presented by the deliverance ministry.

Deliverance – a lay person's guide

The acceptance of the legitimacy of the deliverance ministry for the healing of Christians, and administered by Christians, results from the vexed issue which has concerned the evangelical world in recent years; whether Christians can 'have' a demon. Among neo-Pentecostals the issue is all but settled, with a positive affirmation, although there still remain significant dissenting voices. For the most part, this reverses the earlier teachings by the Classical Pentecostals and conservative evangelicals that it was the unsaved, not 'born-again' Christians, who needed deliverance.

The theological justification for deliverance ultimately stems from the distinction between demonic 'possession' and 'oppression'. In simple terms the argument is that Christians cannot be possessed, that is controlled by an unclean spirit, since this would be a contradiction in terms. Yet, it is possible to be 'oppressed', 'troubled', 'bothered by', 'in bondage to', 'buffeted by', or 'have a demon'. Hence, the spirit of the Christian, the innermost being, is the temple of the Holy Spirit, while the 'outer regions of the believer, that is the body and aspects of the personality, can be demonically "infested".[2] The distinction is not itself particularly original. Roman Catholicism, for instance, has traditionally distinguished between a 'major' and 'lesser' exorcism, as if there were a graduation in the need for demonic expulsion.

All this is very much more than mere theological semantics, but a profound assertion that the demonic may exercise considerable influence over certain aspects of a Christian's life and that this is an inevitable by-product of spiritual warfare. Just as Christians have physical problems like non-Christians, they will also have emotional, psychological and spiritual maladies that will need healing. Various analogies have been advanced. For example, it is as if the Holy Spirit buys a house (the converted Christian), but the woodworm (demons) remain. Deliverance then, is the spiritual Rentokil.

Most academic studies covering deliverance have surveyed the practice within the context of wider studies of spiritual healing almost exclusively concerned with Roman Catholic charismatics. There are few studies that have examined in detail the practice of deliverance, or explored its origins.[3] The roots of the deliverance ministry run deep. Even those involved at an early stage find it difficult to trace its origins, although there is a general myth that it has always existed on the fringe of the Church, carried out by a dedicated minority of activists, perceiving themselves as persecuted by Satan, who wars against those who dare tread on his domain.

As a form of 'lessor exorcism' for Christians, deliverance had its practitioners as early as the 1950s in Britain. Most operated covertly, since they were subject to a great deal of derision and condemnation. The first editions of the books on the subject were literally sold under the counter of some Christian bookshops until the early 1980s. Since then, the popularity and growing respectability of deliverance has been marked by the proliferation of popular works with such exotic titles as, *Evicting Demonic Squatters*, and *Demons Defeated*.

From a broader perspective, the centrality of the practice of deliverance came with the expansion of Pentecostalism and the charismatic movements in the twentieth century. Pentecostalism, in the early decades of the century, developed a strong dualist emphasis on the conflict between good and evil spiritual forces, which gave little room for concerns of the natural world. The influence of a pronounced Pentecostal demonology upon evangelical thought was seen in stark relief in the mission field, and it was from here that the notions of deliverance were understood to refer to the overcoming of demonic powers at the time of conversion. Deliverance was also viewed as a weapon in the 'power encounter' against the cultural influence of pagan deities during the proselytizing endeavour in foreign countries. However, after the great revivals of the early twentieth century, the major Pentecostal bodies came out against the practice of deliverance of Christians and the doctrine that Christians could have demons. The concern with global evangelism enhanced the outward-looking dynamic aspect of the movement and the emphasis put upon the charismata distracted away from the 'beguiling theories of demonism'.[4]

The significant publication which came out of the Pentecostal Welsh Revival in the 1920s within the context of deliverance was Jessie Penn Lewis's *War on the Saints*, which amounts to a rather disturbing and graphic account of demonic infiltration of the body. The work was roundly condemned by the Pentecostal leadership, not only because of its theological implications, but probably out of fear that the doctrine might spread among its uneducated masses. The Pentecostal leaders were also scathing of those on the fringes of the movement who claimed to have a specialized ministry in deliverance on the basis that it drew more attention to Satan than to Christ. Not surprisingly, the enhanced profile and legitimation of deliverance today is causing alarm and has opened up old wounds for the main Pentecostal denominations, as well as their more conservative evangelical critics.[5]

In the 1930s and 40s there were a number of individual Pentecostals for whom theological debates were largely superfluous. Many were linked to the 'Latter Day Rain' movement which arose in the late 1940s and developed a preoccupation with all things demonic. This resulted from the movement's eschatological themes, which stressed that the true Church was under sustained attack by Satanic forces and had to be purified before the imminent second coming of Christ.

This movement was significant because it spawned itinerant quasi-Pentecostal ministries in the 1950s, and in these the charismatic movement almost certainly had some of its origins. They included the ministry of A.A. Allen, a maverick at best and a fraud at worse. With a demonology very close to that of the Latter Day Rain movement, Allen advocated the deliverance of Christians and began to name such demons as 'lust', 'anger' and 'jealousy', and demonic addictions, including 'the spirit of nicotine'. The latter was apparently expelled with a cough and splutter. Of much the same ilk was Oral Roberts, who had strong connections with the emerging charismatic renewal movement in the 1960s and was also the principal link between the deliverance and expanding 'faith movement' of Kenneth Hagin and Kenneth Copeland – both of whom have become renowned for their 'health and wealth' theology.

Another key figure was William Branham, an esoteric figure who claimed to have his own personal guardian angel, and who launched into warfare with demons and diagnosed illness through the colours of auras. Like Allen, he was eventually disowned by the established Pentecostal churches. Two men associated with him at the time were also to become significant in advancing deliverance. One was Ern Baxter, later to become a major advocate of the now discredited 'shepherding' practices. These were identified with stringent control of church members by 'apostles', and were synonymous in Britain with the restoration movement. The other associate of Branham was Paul Cain, the self-designated prophet from a Pentecostal background. Cain was later associated with the ill-reputed Kansas City Prophets, who themselves were eventually absorbed by John Wimber's Vineyard International. Cain also claims to have been inspired by Hobart Freeman, a Faith Minister who produced literature on demonology and the occult, and created controversy in the United States, because of the deaths resulting from his insistence that Christians should not use orthodox medical services.

Then there was the pervading influence of the Fort Lauderdale Five, of which Baxter was a key member. Among them was Don Basham, whose book, *Can Christians Have a Demon?* includes a detailed anecdote of a girl demonically oppressed, outlines her deliverance, considers the need for the deliverance of Christians, and argues that demons should be commanded to name themselves and reveal their 'nature'. Of the Fort Lauderdale Five, however, the principal figure is Derek Prince, who probably brought a greater articulation of the deliverance ministry and accompanying demonology than any other exponent. Most of the leading practitioners today pay tribute to him. Prince pioneered a belief in the hidden dominance of witchcraft in the United States, and talked of demons ordered in a Satanic hierarchy which not only attempted to control human beings, but sought to dominate churches, cities and social and political institutions.

Prince is also largely responsible for maturing the teachings of ancestral spirits and the demonic implication of generational and self-curses on the believer. In Britain, the theology of the Fort Lauderdale Five fed into the restorationist movement, which developed in parallel to mainstream renewal. Indeed, the theme of deliverance had already been explored by early exponents of restorationism, such as Sid Purse and G.W. North. The latter, for example, maintained that symptoms which are commonly recognized as physical, mental, nervous and emotional may have at their roots demonic spirits. In a series of articles, he argued from a strong post-millenarian position that a revival was imminent and for that reason the true Church was being restored and cleansed. A little later, the house churches were to be considerably influenced by some of the other American exponents of deliverance, including Derek Prince.

In mainstream renewal, an early impression was made by the quasi-Pentecostal group, the Full Gospel Business Men's Federation International, which was initially composed of wealthy Pentecostals with a vision for an international missionary enterprise. The federation not only practised the deliverance ministry, but produced copious literature on the subject. The most serious controversy in the early period of the federation involved the public exorcism of Christians, and this was one of the reasons why it was, in the early days, denied access to the American television networks. Nevertheless, the movement grew quickly from the 1970s to the point of infiltrating mainline denominations on both sides of the Atlantic.

The interest in deliverance was further expanded from the early 1980s by the so-called kingdom theology of the 'third wave' movement, with its stress on 'signs and wonders', and the demonstrative power of the Church, which included miraculous healings and deliverance within a strong dualist framework. Implicit here again was the doctrine of 'cleansing the bride of Christ' and 'equipping the saints' – that Christ will return for a Church which is not only spiritually pure and restored as a corporate body, but composed of individuals who are healed and 'demon-free'. One of the leading exponents of the movement, and certainly the most influential, was John Wimber. In his most well-known book, *Power Healing*, he includes an entire chapter on 'Healing the Demonized'.[6] Wimber, in turn, has influenced some of the largest independent deliverance ministries, including Ellel Ministries, which drew media attention by conducting mass deliverance in meetings of several thousands of people, allegedly by invoking the Holy Spirit.

Deliverance and the eschatological imperative

This brief historical survey serves to do more than identify some leading advocates of deliverance. From the Latter-Day movement to that of the Third Wave there have been some common themes that revolve around similar theological outlooks.

Previous academic works have tended to suggest that the different forms of faith-healing furthered by Pentecostal and charismatic groups do not function primarily to reduce medical symptoms. Like other non-Christian forms of spiritual healing, they are principally concerned with reinforcing a belief system. This is especially the case when those beliefs are consonant with a fairly coherent subculture where members tend to view themselves as a beleaguered cognitive minority surrounded by an alien, hostile world. In this sense, many charismatics have their own socially constructed world-view or 'nomos', to use Peter Berger's term.[7] Part of this world-view is a tendency towards a dualist theology in which the practice of deliverance is located and, therefore, appears to be orientated by the higher-order motive of spiritual warfare. At times, this cosmic drama which the theological dualism has precipitated seems to reflect such popular fiction as the film *Star Wars*, and appears to be a legacy of the Cold War. The expulsion of evil spirits, in order to attempt to overcome physical and emotional problems, might appear to be on the fringe of the most fringe of therapies.

Nevertheless, in Christian charismatic circles, the practice is of central importance beyond merely the apparent aim of healing. It is guided by specific eschatological leanings. In charismatic theology, Satan is often perceived as constantly waging war through various strategies, including the 'bondage' of emotional problems, physical illness, ancestral curses and the like, and in doing so supposedly exhausts the energies that each believer should spend in spreading the gospel. To receive deliverance, then, is the duty of Christians and there seems to exist a kind of 'demonic iceberg' of largely hidden Satanic activity into which the unsuspecting believer is likely to sail. Within this paranoid atmosphere, it is not surprising that Penn Lewis's book was eventually re-published.

Another key aspect of the Pentecostal and charismatic healing ministry is the felt necessity to restore a pristine Christianity. This restoration is itself understood to be part of a new divine revelation and the rediscovery of lost practices, of which deliverance is clearly one. There is a fairly widespread view that in these last days, there is a body of knowledge which is being restored by God to the Church at exactly the time that Satanic activity is increasing. It is, therefore, part of the unfolding drama in the struggle between good and evil; where the Church takes the offensive and becomes aware of its spiritual weaponry. It goes without saying that within this context there is a self-enforcing world-view whereby any criticism on the deliverance ministry is interpreted by practitioners as a demonic attack.

While there is undoubtedly a certain 'client' demand for deliverance which may result from a measure of genuine felt need, this demand, to some extent at least, has fed off a heightened awareness of a spiritual conflict and the wider package of demonstrative sign and wonders. If this is so, it is possible that proving the credibility of Christianity in a secular age may well mean that the more immediate needs of Church members are sacrificed to theological expediency.

The principal function of deliverance, then, is linked to the millenarian aspect concerned with cleansing and restoring the Church especially as part of its preparation for the second coming of Christ. This includes freeing it from its perceived legalism, intellectualism and rationalism, which are the result of spiritual oppression. Deliverance becomes a way of 'forcing the end', which is well in tune with the post-millenarian theological legacy, where every demon expelled, whether a territorial spirit dominating a geographical region, or an individual spirit, dominating the believer, is a minus in the demonic ranks of Satan's kingdom.

There is more in this vein to consider. Deliverance, like other forms of spiritual healing, helps to regulate social boundaries. The need to justify themselves as the elect and to demonize the opposition is a common strategy among marginalized cultural and religious groups. Distinguishing your religious community from other cultures usually results in a stringent set of taboos concerning what is, or is not, acceptable behaviour. Ironically, the charismatic movement, which puts so much emphasis on experience, has, through deliverance, become astonishingly legalistic.

For example, if you have experienced trauma or abuse, then demonization invariably and automatically follows. Demons can be transmitted easily within this stringent framework via legitimate moral entrance points. They can enter literally through a human orifice, and they have specific characteristics. Hence, Christians are told not to take off their shoes when visiting a Hindu temple abroad, in case a demon is acquired. Islamic people are literally 'demonized', and said to have the spirit of the anti-Christ, and Sikhs apparently have a spirit of a lion. Spirits of religion are to be found in Jehovah's Witnesses, Mormonism, Christian Science, Christadelphians and anybody else who does not 'belong'.

Like all attempts at boundary maintenance for the true elect, religious or otherwise, sexual taboos figure prominently. Sexual habits need, I am reliably informed, heavy deliverance. Demons, we are told, focus upon genitalia and enter through adultery and fornication, oral sex and homosexuality. If a demon has entered the body because of some sexual sin connected with the mouth, then it is necessary to administer consecrated water or wine. Perhaps it was all too predictable that this would be extended to pouring consecrated wine over the genitalia. With ancestral sins the whole practice becomes quite ludicrous. Those who have not sinned themselves are subject to the repercussions of the actions of their ancestors – hence the young boy delivered of the spirit of adultery because of his grandfather's indiscretion; or the woman delivered of an 'Egyptian god', which was said to have been passed to her because of her great-grandmother's occult practices.

While these inherent aspects of a paranoid world-view are important considerations, it would be simple if the rise of deliverance could be attributed merely to some eschatological wish-fulfilment. Other developments have conspired to bring the practice to the fore. Reinforcing the dualist theological construct of many charismatics has been the arrival of the so-called new religious movements. In the emerging pluralist marketplace of religious beliefs, there are not only the esoteric eastern religions, but occultist practices. During the 1970s, clergymen were administering some kind of psychological or spiritual release from occult and Satanic activities, long before the charismatic movement made deliverance a prominent feature of the healing ministry.

There can be little doubt that the practice of deliverance and exorcism was given respectability by the much-needed Bishop of Exeter's Report (1972) and the work of the Christian Exorcism Study Group.[8] Both the Exeter Report and the CESG portrayed a picture of clergy largely baffled over how to deal with parishioners disturbed by the occult activities in which they had become ensnared.

In this sense, the recommendations of the CESG brought the Church into the modern world by confronting head-on the issues of the day, rather than retreating into the Dark Ages. However, Stephen Pattison, in his book on healing (which is surely one of the best among those flooding the market) makes the point that while such reports are scholarly and authoritative, they have also had unfortunate effects.[9] The danger is that they give credence to the trivialized and widespread use of deliverance in charismatic circles and feed the paranoid world-view of some deliverance practitioners.

Consumer demand

There are other good reasons why deliverance cannot merely be dismissed as a throwback to the rampant superstition of the Middle Ages. Paradoxically, there is something very modern about it and, even more so, something desperately middle class. Of course, no religion is immune from the effects of the wider socio-economic and cultural context in which it is located. Consciously or unconsciously, modern religious beliefs and practices are the repository of social values and contemporary changes in the secular world. In the marketplace of religion, where religious groups compete against each other for members, there are growth sectors within the churches which mobilize resources, including fashionable consumer articles in attractive packages.

At first glance, there might appear to be little which is attractive about deliverance. There is, however, a flourishing market. Although the framework in which deliverance operates is essentially theological, there is clearly a great deal which is profoundly secular and clearly exploits developments in the modern world. This is consonant with the great strength of the charismatic movement in being 'world-accommodating' in its nature. While in many respects the movement is theologically 'fundamentalist' (the term itself being open to interpretation), it simultaneously accommodates and exploits contemporary fashions and trends. More specifically, it taps the modern preoccupation with health, human potential and experience, albeit transformed, 'spiritualized' and embraced within its own world-view.

Hence, while some of the movement's adherents may believe they are retreating into a safe subculture, they are, ironically, very much enmeshed in the world and caught up in the cultural modes of the late twentieth century. From one perspective, the attractions of charismatic renewal have always appeared to dovetail well with familiar middle-class cultural attributes and aspirations, namely the pursuit of self-fulfilment and experience as a form of consumerism, which are channelled into a privatized religious quest. Glossalalia, prophecy, being slain in the spirit, Toronto twitches and the like are, in many respects, part of the same cultural mood that has its clear religious trajectories.

While ecstatic expressions of the faith have been factors accounting for the success of classical Pentecostalism, there are good grounds for suggesting that through neo-Pentecostalism they are transferred to an increasingly middle-class acceptance of emotional expression as part of everyday life. Such ecstatic expression brings to the fore what had previously been stigmatized, and it marks an attempt to liberate inhibitions and legitimate emotional release. Implicit here is a calculated hedonism, engaging a more aesthetic and emotional exploration, and where the child-like adult now has greater licence to explore emotions and act spontaneously.

Since the 1960s, there has been a relaxation of emotional controls and an exploration of the feelings which were formerly forbidden and accompanied by strong interpersonal and psychic sanctions. The result is an all-pervading, narcissistic emotional exploration and relationship-building ambience, at the expense of public and communal concerns. In simple terms, there is a preoccupation with sensory experience, where the modern consumer is expected to be permanently unsatiated and seething with desire for new experiences and pleasures.

To some extent, this search for subjective experience marks a reaction to a previous over-regulation of the body. The body itself has now become almost a consumer object – the basis of pleasure, indulgence and the desire to 'be in your own body'. From a sociological perspective, the body is a cultural object controlled and perceived in culturally-defined ways, and is linked to structured systems of meaning. Until relatively recently, evangelical attitudes to the body had been strait-laced and restrained, to say the least. Christians were expected to be vigilant and in constant control of their bodies and emotions, which were 'for the Lord'. Hence, traditional inner-worldly asceticism included negative attitudes about the 'self' – namely, self-denial and self-discipline.

These attitudes towards the body weakened in the 1960s with profound cultural – and indeed, counter-cultural – changes, which filtered through fundamentalist beliefs. Sickness was once something which could be regarded as a sign of divine election, by which the righteous could be purified and perfected. On the other hand, the deeply-rooted Christian symbolism underlining the frailty and eventual decay of the human body was a metaphor for sin and natural depravity. But no longer. Physical, emotional and psychological problems must be overcome. Evangelical charismatics have increasingly adopted a positive and holistic view of the human person, in contrast to earlier, pessimistic conceptions that devalued the body and treated it like a dangerous machine. This is reflected in the holistic orientation of charismatic healing ministry. Deliverance is one such expression of the 'liberated' body, but like the drug ecstasy, there is within it an endless, never-satisfied search for experience. It is little wonder that there has developed the phenomenon of the 'deliverance fix' whereby individuals become obsessed with the whole process and the personal attention which it affords.

All of this amounts to a rejection of rationalism, which is imposed upon every aspect of private as well as public life, where even for the middle classes, employment has become more routine and mechanized, more alienating. Even the charismatic theology, such as it is, has its compensatory attractions by encouraging escapist fantasies. The 'epistemological individualism' of the contemporary world tends to give people the perceived capabilities of not only discovered 'reality' and 'truth', but of creating them symbolically and experimentally through religious constructs. The individual Church member is given a sense of personal participation in the shaping of a utopian future, a feeling of worth, power and triumphalism, while simultaneously reshaping the self-image. All this fits well with the optimism of post-millennialism, in which the feeling of facing unjust opposition, real or perceived, Satanic or worldly, has a certain appeal, and where the hope of revival is transformed into an inevitability.

Christian healing among the middle classes is part of a general trend towards alternative therapy embraced by the more educated, acculturated and economically secure people. Unlike the charismatic movement, the lower class and black ethnic basis of classical Pentecostalism has had no interest in emotional healing, no middle-class preoccupation with all things therapeutic. Hence, Christian healing centres and courses on deliverance are largely filled by a middle-class clientele, with typically middle-class complaints.

There is good reason to suggest that deliverance is largely derived from Christian counselling and techniques of 'inner healing', feeding off the so-called psychotherapeutic revolution, which itself has attributes of a religious system. It should not be too surprising to note that many of the leading practitioners of deliverance had begun in counselling and forms of psychotherapy. There are times when the deliverance ministry looks more like group encounter therapy or some other form of 'spiritualized psychotherapy' – perhaps the 'rebirth' techniques of the Christian psychologist Frank Lake, subsequently given a 'demonic gloss', or the use of group processes as ways of acting out feelings through psycho-drama. There are also 'optional extras'. If public deliverance is not to one's taste one can even indulge in a more advanced course of 'self-deliverance'.[10]

Invariably, there exist profound theological and sociological repercussions. In many Christian psychotherapeutic techniques, a definite shift can be seen from the virtues of suffering to the preoccupation with healing. When there are calls for the development of human potential, for personal fulfilment and holistic lifestyles, the root of sin is perceived as being tied to anger, fear and anxiety, instead of the breaking of religious laws. Salvation is reduced to simple steps, easy procedures and formulas for psychological rewards, and religious truth shifts away from any objective grounds to a more subjective, more instrumental understanding of what it does for the believer.

I was once invited to a deliverance training weekend in which charismatic Christians were meant to discover how to conduct deliverance in their own churches. Learning was done by a process of 'self-discovery' via the application of formulas. There were demons of sexual abuse cast out in the morning, occultist demons after lunch, and phobias after dinner. The next two days had their own extensive programmes. Deliverance for beginners in easy steps. There was something for everyone: demons of rejection, frustrated careers, buggery, nail-biting, and demons of lumpy custard.

Half of those on the course had attended in previous years and were just participating in their own deliverance 'fix'. My impression was that it was all rather self-indulgent. Everyone knew what to expect and performed accordingly. It amounted to an opportunity for people to let their hair down and have a 'damn good scream' – all quite therapeutic. There was a lot of frantic shaking and rolling around the floor, playing out collective hysteria and personal tantrums. By the end of the course, during which practically everyone had been delivered of one demon or another, an Anglican woman noticing my inactivity turned to me and said: 'You appear to have got through your Christian life remarkably unscathed.'

Power and its abusers

The concept of 'medicalization' is a term given to describe the ever-growing power of the orthodox medical profession and medical agencies, and in particular, the range of social activities which have come under their legitimate auspices. Within this context, one perennial concern is the way scientific medicine has come to bring inside its remit social deviance which is deemed to be in need of 'controlling'. This appears to be a particular function of psychiatry. Since contemporary religious groups can carry the ideologies of orthodox medicine, and deliverance appears to have close parallels with this medical specialism, it should not be surprising that deliverance conforms to psychiatric categories and confronts supposed 'social deviants' in much the same way.

The 'anti-psychiatry' debate which emerged in the 1960s pointed out how psychiatry was becoming an instrument of social control. Some exponents of this critical school even declared that there is no such thing as mental illness at all. Rather, they said, psychiatry constitutes the twentieth-century equivalent of medieval witch-hunts, and psychiatrists, in their search for the signs and symptoms of psychopathology in patients, are the direct descendants of those inquisitors who interrogated their victims for the sinister signs of demoniacal possession.

The metaphors should not be lost on us. Mental illness can be seen as a social construct and a powerful label to use against those who do not conform to accepted models of behaviour. In Illich's scathing attack upon the medical profession, this form of labelling is ironically referred to as 'naming the spirit' that undermines deviance, thereby placing the deviant under the control of the powers that be. Psychiatry then, appeared to do little more than engage itself in the sterile collecting, naming and classifying of arbitrarily defined psychological phenomena. It merely constituted a character assassination of those suspected of not belonging, while denigrating and ridiculing their vivid, subjective experiences.

Schizophrenia is a good instance. Very often this category of mental illness has been used by totalitarian regimes as a label for those who do not conform. The interesting aspect of this alleged psychiatric complaint is that as a medical classification it is a relatively recent 'discovery'. In fact, many societies have no comprehension of such a form of mental illness. Moreover, those who have studied people labelled as having schizophrenia have even maintained that no such thing may exist at all.

The irony is that demonic categories conform very closely to the models of medical science, and therefore inherit all the limitations of medical science, including its stigmatizing labels. There are demons of alcoholism, child abuse, opiate addiction, obesity and problems with sexual functioning. The eating disorders of anorexia and bulimia are treated in this way. The former is essentially viewed as a spirit of suicide, self-hate, or self-destruction, manifested as suicide by starvation. With bulimia, the origins are said to include the spirit of 'the fear of starvation', along with a 'little girl spirit' – where the woman is trapped in some childhood state as a result of a past emotional trauma.

It may be difficult to agree that discerning people with evil spirits is a stigmatizing process, but in many respects that is exactly what is does. This is particularly the case if the process also carries cultural ideas of what are, or are not, acceptable forms of behaviour. Many deliverance ministries identify demons of specific mental complaint which copy the western classifications. Schizophrenia is a common one.

We are told that schizophrenia is really a nest of demon spirits, clustering around the core demons of rejection and rebellion. One has to ask: rebellion against what? Once diagnosed as mentally ill, the patient is by definition in no position to argue against the stigmatizing label. In much the same way, anyone said to be oppressed by a demon is in no position to argue otherwise. Perhaps more obviously it must be questioned as to whether deliverance practitioners really contribute a great deal by designating specific medical complaints as 'demons'. Those with acute emotional and psychological maladies are unlikely to be helped if they are told that they are also demonized.

The ultimate expression of deliverance is what I have heard referred to as the 'trawling technique'. This means treating all illnesses and personal problems as demonic, and conducting deliverance with the rationale that if evil spirits are present, they will be dealt with; if no demons are present, no harm will be done. This kind of thinking encourages the view that all emotional and psychological problems are demonic. Deliverance becomes the cure-all for each and every condition, which ultimately leads to an unnecessary intrusion into a person's private life. This can cause serious psychological damage in itself when what may be needed is other forms of pastoral care.[11]

There is another parallel with psychiatry. Christian healing methods generally tend to be individualistic in their scope. In many respects, this reflects the prevailing economic ethos in the West of consumerism and consumer choice. Lifestyles are seen as a matter of choice and individual responsibility. This cultural element is one step away from the individual being perceived as morally responsible for their condition of illness. Plausibly, this is why deliverance practitioners speak endlessly of legitimate 'moral gateways' which permit demonic entrance.

In psychiatry, there are a variety of approaches to mental health problems. Many practitioners put their faith in the belief that disorders rest upon a physical basis, rather than considering an assessment of personal relationships and wider causes such as poverty, unemployment, inequality, discrimination, racism and other social origins. Deliverance often operates within similar parameters. Some physical disorders are said to be caused by demons linked to ancestral curses and emotional bondage, which cause stomach disorders, headaches and tumours. While we should not discount a link between the psychological and biological, which is typified by psychosomatic conditions, there is still the danger of holding the individual ultimately responsible for the causes of ailments outside of his or her control.

In discussing the above points, we have only really skirted around the key issue, which is surely one of power. In psychiatry, considerable power rests with the psychiatrist. His or her relationship with the patient is not just a therapeutic association, but also an authoritative relationship. Part of this power derives from the process of diagnosis. Even in secular group therapeutic techniques, there are authoritative tendencies in terms of hierarchical organization, structure, ritual, levels of commitment and charismatic leaders. Even in the least authoritarian healing group, and despite the best of intentions, there is a tendency for individuals to have a large controlling influence. Personal qualities and group dynamics appear to produce a longing for leadership that exposes members to high levels of suggestibility.

An air of mystery and mystique surrounds the secular and religious healing practitioner. He or she is seen as a special, charismatic individual, with perceived qualities beyond the command of others. Those conducting deliverance have much to learn from some of the problems emerging from the practitioner-client relationship in psychiatry in terms of suggestion, persuasion and manipulation. Sadly, the unscrupulous have already learned how to take advantage of these lessons. Only they know if you have a demon; only they know if there is one more to come out. Cross-culturally, the faith-healer, whatever his precise remit, has some merit in dealing with the whole person, physical, emotional and spiritual, but this also constitutes a clear difficulty. Deliverance means passing control of the whole person – mind, body and soul – to those conducting the deliverance process. It is ultimately the source of abuse in deliverance, since it weaves deep relationships of reliance and trust, rendering the weak vulnerable to the exploitation of the fanatical.

The recourse to various forms of spiritual healing may be regarded as an attempt to gain power on the part of those who do not have any, and a way of exerting social influence for those who practise it. Conducting deliverance may provide some people with the status they lack in secular life. Without wishing to draw too strong a parallel, it might be worth noting that in Sri Lanka, the Buddhist exorcists are of a fairly low social caste. They gain greater prestige through conducting rites of exorcism. This allows them a way of increasing their social status, and for this reason they are usually avoided by the upper castes.[12]

Historical accounts of possession and exorcism in the late sixteenth and early seventeenth centuries in France and England seem to suggest that those who were allegedly possessed or obsessed by the demonic were often taught how to behave by the exorcist – and this has a parallel with the psychiatrist dealing with the mentally ill. In both fields, the ritual serves to confirm the beliefs and status of those who exercise it. In the atmosphere which over-emphasizes the demonic, there is considerable pressure for individuals to 'perform'. In a sense, there has always existed a flip-side to the charismatic movement: rather than providing a haven for emotional release, it has long been concerned with individuals conforming by 'feeling correctly'. Those who have attended deliverance meetings will be aware of the curious and often disturbing physical manifestations which can occur. Some useful insights were provided in 1930 by T.K. Oesterreich, a Christian who wrote about Christian and non-Christian ecstatic religion in the context of demonic oppression. He argued that a great deal of what he observed resulted from suggestion. In particular, he said that the belief in the existence of evil spirits encouraged psychic experiences, which in turn were interpreted as demonic possession. The apparent transcendental encounters tended to confirm the validity of pre-existing religious ideas.[13]

Religious beliefs include elements of faith or trust in the spiritual power, which usually includes perceptions of cause and effect in the world, and how the supernatural impinges upon it. In charismatic interpretations of religion, concepts of power have a central role and function. Power brings a level of explanation, predictability, and attempted control of the world and, thereby, holds together and enhances the belief system.

The charismatic movement, with its emphasis on spiritual gifts, ensures that extra-human powers, rather than science and reason, have become the critical reference points for interpreting daily life. However, when the power integral to religious belief converges with secular notions of power, it can become particularly dynamic and, unfortunately, sometimes disastrous. Modern culture puts considerable emphasis upon social, economic and political aspects of 'power'. This is especially so in a competitive market, where power is closely linked to aspirations for success. When this is transferred to the religious sphere, there is a relentless drive for showmanship and triumphalism, of which deliverance, particularly in its collective displays, is so much a part.

In weighing up some of these dimensions of power, it may be possible that in the case with some go-it-alone deliverance ministries, we may be speaking about the development of a cult. Theologically, it is often argued that if a religious group puts undue emphasis on particular peripheral doctrines, then it might be legitimate to speak of a cult. The term 'cult', however, is an awkward one. Sociologically, the term 'sect' is preferred if the reference is also to a religious collective, with a strong charismatic leader who is perceived to be imbued with special powers. This claim may at first appear to be a little harsh. There are undoubtedly honest practitioners among such itinerant ministries, but there also others who have neither wisdom nor virtue, and for whom the esoteric 'gift of discernment of spirits' operates as a perverted ego-trip.

Historically, the area of exorcism has always been exercised with discretion, in that it has been kept within the remit of ecclesiastic authority. The position in the Church of England at the time of the Reformation was in practice not very different from that of the Roman Catholic Church. Formal permission for exorcism was required by the bishop, but in practice this was rarely exercised. I would suggest that this was not merely because of the malevolent spiritual powers believed to be confronted, but also because of the potential misuse of power by those conducting the ritual.

In considering the above points, the word 'accountability' comes to mind. In most of the mainline denominations, lines of accountability exist. Unfortunately, abuses occur in spite of them, as is evident in recent cases. Moreover, the authority commanded by deliverance practitioners is derived from informal relationships and their supposed personal qualities, not from their position in ecclesiastical hierarchies.

At the end of the day, academic critiques, which this work purports to be, are all well and good. Yet, there is more at the common sense level. Surely, there is something profoundly unhealthy about this obsession with the demonic. I think that it might be justified to speak theologically of 'majoring in minors'. Christianity is surely a religion of light, and not of darkness.

4

Healing Ministries and their Potential for Harm

Russ Parker

Before examining some of the possible harmful effects found in some practices of the Christian healing ministry, I would like to address what we understand by Christian healing. It is in a misunderstanding of this that the first harm can occur, because so much of the process and style of ministry we offer, as well as the effect we will have upon our clients, will be a reflection of what we believe and expect to happen. Our understanding of healing acts as the foundational building block in our structures of care and practice. Consequently, it is imperative that we have a balanced acquaintance of the basics of what constitutes Christian healing.

This is especially necessary now with the increased high profile of the healing ministry within the major Church denominations. Approximately one third of all Anglican churches now have some form of healing ministry as part of their regular ministry. A recent survey of the churches in Liverpool Diocese revealed that over fifty per cent have a healing service. Alongside this there has been the explosion of the prayer ministry cum counselling approach to healing of the charismatic fellowships. In this country now, far more churches are likely to be involved in some form of healing than they are in evangelistic mission.

Consequently, it is extremely important that we have a proper understanding of what Christian healing is and form an appropriate practice of engaging with it. In a BBC *Everyman* documentary shown in 1995, it was stated that the rise in healing ministry was a result of the Toronto Blessing. This is quite inaccurate, as the charismatic or Pentecostal contribution to healing is a comparatively new arrival in this field, although it continues to exert an ever-increasing influence in ministry styles. The fostering of Christian healing was pioneered in this country by societies such as the Guild of St Raphael, the Guild of Health, the Order of St Luke and the Acorn Christian Healing Trust. Parallel to this has been the much-valued work of the Churches Council for Health and Healing, which was the vision of Archbishop William Temple, and is especially concerned to build bridges of mutual resourcing and co-operation between medicine and healing.

However, with the advent of charismatic renewal, the climate of Christian healing has significantly altered. Before this event, the healing ministry was a relatively quiet and unnoticed affair as far as the media and general public were concerned. However, the healing ministry has now become much more of a marketplace ministry than the prerogative of the specialist and this is both to be welcomed as well as to be properly supervised and made accountable. It is to this latter development that the remainder of this paper is addressed.

Before continuing, let me point out that I shall be using two terms to describe the relationship between the one seeking healing and the one offering healing. They are respectively 'client' and 'therapist'. In using these terms I am not making direct comparisons with the medical or psychotherapeutic fraternities, but only using them for the sake of clarity of relationships.

What is Christian healing?

At the core of Pentecostal encounter is a focus on the power of God to act within human experience and need. This has very much coloured the popular understanding of what constitutes Christian healing. Healing is all too easily defined as curing when in reality it is far more complex than this. However, such a view raises all kinds of questions for those who do not recover from their illnesses, as well as for those who minister to them. It is precisely at this point that so many clients are re-abused by their would-be therapists. They may be told that their faith is not strong enough, or that they are harbouring some sin in their lives, or, more seriously, that there is some demonic spirit which has gained access to their lives through their family background or through their own lifestyle.

I do not doubt that there may well be occasions when these factors are true for certain clients and that they are usually arrived at after engaging in a proper recognition procedure, in which the client supplies the information rather than being told of a possible road block within their lives. However, far too often these charges are made when we are desperate to maintain our commitment to a narrow view of healing, rather than to accept the reality of mystery, suffering and not knowing why some recover and others do not.

Like Job's comforters, when our client does not respond to treatment and advice, we react with alleged inside information about their problematic lives. The best thing which Job's counsellors did for him was their first discipline, which was to sit silently beside him and 'behold' his awful condition. This gave Job the creative space to do what happened next in his story, which was to open his mouth and give voice to his complaint and pain. Yet this was too strong meat for his helpers, who felt threatened by a 'client' who was clearly criticizing God for letting his sickness and suffering happen. There is a real sense in which Job represents the healer's or counsellor's greatest nightmare. That is when the client says to his therapist, 'I tried that but it didn't work!' Job's counsellors defended themselves by inflicting on Job their well-tuned theology, but delivered with total insensitivity or accuracy to Job's condition.

What effect does this kind of response have upon the client? All too often it leads to introspection and an ever-spiralling downwards in search of that one issue which holds up the process of healing. As a by-product, it makes the client unhealthily dependent upon the therapist, to whom has come the responsibility for discovering the fault and delivering the healing. The dangers of this kind of authoritarianism are never more real than in the area of deliverance ministry. If after receiving prayer, the distress or malady continues, too often it is suggested that there is some other, more stronger demon at work. This is because strong emotions and distressing behaviour patterns are all too simply misread as demonic influence.

I well remember being invited to counsel a woman while I was staying at a healing centre, and being informed that she was severely demonized and that the prayer ministry she had received had not effected a cure. With a female member of staff, I spent a little time with this person who shared a distressing story of marital stress in which her husband refused to practise birth control of any kind. Consequently, she was continually pregnant with a growing number of children to look after.

For her part, she longed to return to paid employment, but her condition frustrated her hopes. When she conveyed this to her husband, she was told that she was being awkward and rebellious and needed prayer. She complied with his demands and this made her feel very angry indeed. This was interpreted as a spirit of anger, but deliverance ministry only made matters worse and she had become very destructive in her behaviour towards the family. Her counsellors had told her that there was a hierarchy of demons operating in her life and that they all needed to be removed if she was going to be 'cured'.

Instead of offering further deliverance, I listened to her story and reflected back that on the one hand she felt angry because her wishes were being ignored, and that on the other she had been told that she needed setting free from demonic power. Then I invited her to choose what action she now wished to take, to explore her angry feelings or the possibility of a demonic hold upon her life. She expressed surprise that she did in fact have a choice of what to do. She elected to explore her feelings and this resulted in confronting her husband's unreasonable behaviour and making him hear her story properly and probably for the first time. Because he listened and understood, it changed her attitude and feelings overnight. Because he truly heard her complaint, it re-energized her. Later on,

I was asked by one of the team members at the conference centre what was the spirit I had cast out of her, because she was so much better. I replied by saying that I simply listened to her feelings, and that by respecting them and giving her the opportunity to explore them, she was enabled to take responsibility for managing her life to some degree.

With the preoccupation of healing as curing, we fail to make room for woundedness, vulnerability and the fact that healing is more often a process or journey into wholeness rather than an instant cure. The World Health Organization defines health as 'a state of complete physical, mental and social well-being and not merely the absence of disease or infirmity'. According to this definition, we would be hard-pressed indeed to find anyone in the world who is healthy! However, it does at least point to the fact that healthiness is not just physical well-being but personal well-being. Therefore, a better way of understanding the content of healing is that of care for the whole person, rather than the cure of a presenting problem or malady.

This is borne out by the context and character of Jesus' healing work. In virtually every passage of the Gospels which describe Jesus' healing acts, the context is given as the preaching of the gospel or the announcing of the coming of the kingdom of God (Matthew 4:23-25; Luke 9:1-6). In other words, healing is never an end in itself, nor is it to be conducted separately from a concern for the spiritual well-being of the other. Elsewhere we read of the healing of the woman with internal bleeding (Luke 8:42-48) and that of the ten lepers (Luke 17:11-20). In both accounts, Jesus focuses attention not on their physical healing, but on their openness to God which is what truly made them whole or healthy. Before their expression of devotion, they were merely healed of their physical problem, but now they were made whole because they had turned to God. William Tyndale, in his version of the Bible, translated the word *soteria*, usually rendered as 'salvation' or 'save', to mean 'health' or 'healing'. Therefore, the words of Jesus to the repentant Zacchaeus become: 'Today health has come into this house' (Luke 19:9).

Another bad effect upon the client, if we narrow healing down to curing, is that the unhealed often feel abandoned and unsupported in their on-going sickness. They have nowhere to go and mistakenly believe that because they have not been cured they have had no measure of healing from God. Yet it is plain that the New Testament view of healing embraces a much wider concept. There are the healing issues of forgiveness and reconciliation, which all too often have to be followed by the hard work of living out a renewed relationship. There is growing in peace and love, with the challenge to holiness as well as wholeness of life. Quite often, Jesus' care of another would include the therapy of simply listening and being in touch with the distressed, as was the case with Cleopas and his friend on the Emmaus Road (Luke 24:14-35).

I am challenged by the question of Dr Sheila Cassidy in her book, *Sharing the Darkness*, when she writes of the dying Jesus at Calvary. There is Jesus on the cross, screaming out his pain and asking why God had abandoned him – and of course, the 'why' questions are always the hardest to answer when there is no healing. Yet Jesus' mother and a few friends hear his scream. Cassidy asks, 'What can they do to make Jesus feel better and heal his agony?'[1] Her answer is twofold: firstly, nothing, and secondly, be there. The place of powerlessness in the face of ongoing sickness is very difficult for the therapist who sees healing as just curing. Yet these two gifts of empathetic care are the very healing requirements needed if we would give strength to the weak. Perhaps the knowledge that others were in touch with his pain, but not able to cure, is what gave Jesus the strength to do the next thing – and that was to move on in his journey with God.

Healing very often means being the presence of God to another in their sickness, and so enabling them to grow in grace and see this as a dimension of healing. This is often the testimony of palliative care, when there is no reasonable expectation of recovery, but only the expectation of death. Bereavement itself needs to be taken seriously as a necessary aspect of the healing journey and not something to be brushed aside with shallow praise and prayer.

I have always remembered the words of a friend and fellow minister who gave the address at his wife's funeral. He had agonized and cried to God to explain to him why his wife had died so horribly in a car crash when she was only twenty-six years old. He had received no answers to his hard questions. However, he had reminded himself of the fact that Jesus also had died a horrible death but rose again, and that some day Christ would return and then he would be reunited with his wife in the heavenly glory. He concluded his talk with these words: 'I do not know why God let my wife die in this way, but what I do know (of Jesus) helps me to live with what I don't know.' Surely an aspect of our healing ministry is to help people live with what they do not know and not offer some cheap explanation? We must not imprison people in a fruitless search for the answer to why they are not cured, but provide them with care to grow and move on with their lives.

Now let us examine some of the inherent dangers in the practice of the healing ministry itself. First we will look at some of the dynamics in the relationship between the therapist and client, and then we will go on to conclude with some discussion on various popular issues currently prevalent in the healing ministry.

The dynamics between client and therapist

Very often people come to receive prayer for healing in a very vulnerable state. They are seeking a cure for their sickness and carry the hope and expectation that the therapist will have the faith and knowledge to help them. In the prayer-counselling styles of healing ministry, this can often lead to disclosures of a deeply personal nature, as the therapist asks more and more probing questions before engaging in prayer. This can be all the more harmful when we realize that the one praying has often had no training in counselling and can often open up wounded emotions with little idea about how to hold them appropriately and thus prevent ongoing leakage of painful feelings after the time of ministry is over. More than one client has gone away from having received healing prayer feeling more vulnerable. Often they have been filled with fear and depression because they have opened up some deep problem which has been cheaply prayed for, but the problem remains – only now it feels worse, because they have shared it to no useful advantage.

Part of the problem of course is that the client may be feeling distressed and is looking for a short route to cure, avoiding the often harder work of systematically working through all the issues with which they struggle. This is less attractive than the power of prayer to heal them without laborious work. Interestingly enough, one of the comments emerging from people who have been impacted with the Toronto Blessing is that they feel the blessing they received was like compressing into a moment what would have formerly taken a lengthy period of counselling or personal growth work. While I do not wish to undermine any true blessing which another has received, I can see the dangerous attraction of looking upon charismatic ministry as an alternative to confronting and working through personal growth difficulties.

Another danger in this dynamic is that the client invests the one praying with a greater access to God's power, simply because they are in the place of need and the therapist is in the place of helping. Jane Pooley and David Wood call this process the re-introjection of the idealized leader in the life of the vulnerable.[2] They maintain that the weak always need a hero or an idol, whom they invest with the authority and power to help them. It is precisely here that they see the seeds of the formation of a cult, from the Latin *cultus*, which itself is derived from *colere*, meaning 'to worship'. With the giving away of responsibility to the therapist, and the parallel investing of authority and guidance over their life, the client is open to a range of abuses.

The therapist, on the other hand, can find this kind of scenario very tempting, and if there is no proper supervision and accountability for their healing ministry, they can fall to the temptation to play the game of guru to their client. One of the ways that this is manifested within the charismatic world is the use of what I will call inappropriate or bogus 'words of knowledge'. While I fully appreciate the value and place of this charism (which involves being given an understanding of a subject from God's perspective), far too often such words are but the hunches and opinions of the one praying. Often there is no procedure for verifying or checking out the words once given. Yet they are given on the understanding that they will be accepted and acted upon. This can be quite dangerous.

For example, some clients share the difficulties they have had with their sexuality and personal relationships. When they go on to say that they cannot remember much before a certain age in their childhood, the therapist often says that God has shown them that this is because they were abused by a parent in their childhood. Because the client is needy for understanding and is vulnerable, this so-called revelation is firmly believed. Tragically, what follows for some is an increasingly bizarre story of ritualized abuse by one or both parents, and a complete breakdown of the family unit. A corollary to this is that the client is absorbed into the life of the Church, because having lost one family they now require a replacement family. It is because of this abuse of the healing dynamic that false-memory syndrome has emerged, where clients are now confessing that the memories they formerly believed in were only in response to the convictions and suggestions of their therapists.

How then can we protect the client-therapist dynamic from degenerating into a harmful scenario? Bishop Morris Maddocks, the Adviser on Healing to the Archbishops of Canterbury and York, writes that the one in the place of healer should always follow the example of Jesus, who modelled the role of servant to others' needs.[3] He quotes Archbishop Donald Coggan, who said that the very name 'Jesus' came from an Aramaic word which meant 'to be spacious'.[4] In other words, by serving another, we given them space and responsibility to choose what they share and what they will do with this. It was Henri Nouwen who said that space is the offer of hospitality in which change can take place. Jesus comes as a shepherd rather than a Lord. He teaches us not to be possessive of

73

those who seek out our care and ministry, and always to free them to choose, in the hope that they will do so wisely.

Secondly, it would be helpful to keep public prayers for healing shorter, rather than developing them into a counselling session. Counselling and ministry are two quite different enterprises and should not be confused. Although this is an artificial boundary to make, it actually helps to distinguish between two different disciplines. Far too many Christians use the term for counselling as their healing function when they really mean ministry. Most of these so-called counsellors have received no formal training, are seldom supervised and receive no supervision for their work. Counselling is a highly-disciplined, skills-based technique of caring, according to which school of counselling one may be committed. It is usually client-centred and has as its main function a process of empowering the client to clarify their problems and needs. Once this is achieved, the client then decides upon their chosen action.

Counselling is often that work of clarification which can help decide the appropriate form of ministry that may need to follow. Ministry, therefore, is very directive and should be minimized and not intrude into the private world of the client. Ministry should concentrate on listening, in order to help the other person decide what they wish to share, and in order to focus prayer largely upon this. Should there be a need of going deeper and further into the problems of the client, then it should be delegated to those who are trained for this work. Just as the counselling world is being increasingly scrutinized in order to achieve excellence, perhaps the processes of healing ministry should equally be scutinized and made accountable.

Another helpful factor would be to incorporate some forms of prayer ministry that are non-disclosing. This is where the person is prayed for without being asked their need, and the prayers offered are usually short and of a single sentence duration. If the model of the New Testament Gospel writers is a clue to anything, it seems that the prayers of Jesus were usually quite short and very sharply focused on the request of his clients.

Finally, each person engaged in praying for healing should never do this in isolation or without accountability to someone else. This is surely a reminder that we are all wounded healers and carry our own needs too. It helps us to remember that we are not called into this ministry because we are the strong and the well, but because we are simply called to care for one another, just as Christ cared for us. He was the most wounded healer of us all.

Popular issues with potential harm

The following items are just some of the assumptions and attitudes which I perceive in popular belief surrounding the healing ministry today. As such, they influence the advice and care we give to others, and in some circumstances the results have been tragic.

The difference between prayer and promise – Too many times I have heard preachers rehearse the healings of Jesus and then go on to say that Jesus is still able to heal today as he did in the days of his first advent. So far I have no quarrel with this argument. However, they then go on to say that therefore Jesus will heal you today if you will only believe in him. In other words, they are promising healing to another when in fact we have no such mandate to say this in the New Testament. This is not quite the same thing as praying for healing and hoping and expecting God to heal. When we promise healing, we are giving a guarantee that healing will follow, and to be perfectly honest, this is not the case in over 50 per cent of those seeking healing. Consequently, we appear to be fraudulent in our ministry and undermine the value of the healing care of others.

Some preachers promise healing, perhaps in the hope that it will raise and release faith in the seeker and that consequently more healing will follow. Consider, for example, the promise made by Morris Cerullo in more than one of his London Healing Crusades that 'you will see miracles'. This attracted such media attention that when they tried to inspect the nature of the healings being claimed, it resulted in a diminishing of the healing help which some had actually received (because they were not dramatic miracles), and devalued the whole healing ministry in the eyes of the public.

I am quite sure that there are times, when we pray for someone's healing, that we receive a God-given conviction that they are going to be healed. However, this is not the time to draw attention to the therapist, but to use such insight to lend conviction to our praying. How many disappointed people are there who have been told that they were going to be healed but were not? They often feel bitterly disappointed and disillusioned by the Church, and some also lose their faith. I think it is perfectly reasonable to pray with as much conviction of heart as we possess for another's recovery and then to leave our hope in the hands of God, for he is free to do what he will with our prayers and needs. It is not our place to promise what God has not first revealed to us by his Spirit.

Medicine and healing – One of the dangers I see in the healing ministry is to view with suspicion anyone who goes to see their doctor after receiving healing prayer. It is regarded as a failure of faith or a rival to the efficacy of prayer. Consequently, a number of people have been urged to 'trust in the Lord' and throw away their pills or medication. Some years ago, I had a parishioner who we shall call Penny, who was taking regular medication for her stressful psychological condition. At a healing service which she attended out of town, she was pronounced whole in Christ. She was then encouraged to show her trust and belief in God by doing away with her injections, as this was considered to be a bad reflection on God's ability to heal. This she did and for a few days seemed quite radiant and pleased. However, her joy soon became manic and her behaviour patterns began to fragment and she ended up screaming outside the vicarage at four in the morning. Sadly, she had to be sectioned for a short time before returning home. However, this was not the greatest damage to Penny. For some months afterwards, she was consumed with guilt for letting the Lord down for not being healed.

I think it is high time that those of us engaged in the healing ministry should appreciate the need for drug-based medication for certain psychological conditions and stress-filled circumstances. Far from regarding such medication as the enemy, we should at least commit such treatment to God and where necessary pray for the removal of any unnecessary side effects.

Partly behind this kind of polarization in the healing ministry is the inability to appreciate that God's healing care is equally present in the learned skills and abilities of others as well as in the prayers of the faithful. Within the Acorn Christian Healing Trust, we have long encouraged people with medical training to team up with others who have pastoral and healing gifts and to find some expression of working together to show a more complete model of Christ the healer. It must also be said that the medical fraternity has not helped matters by its own suspicions and antipathy towards the Church's ministry of healing, and the orthodox ministries associated with it. This matter is even more complicated by the growing association of the British Medical Association with alternative therapies – including the Christian healing ministry.

Therefore we need a balanced approach to medicine, and perhaps this is where the model of Jesus is once again so helpful. Almost as a matter of routine or policy, after he prayed for healing, he would encourage his clients to go and see the high priest to have their healing checked out. In this way, they could be pronounced clean and return to full involvement in the community. It seems to me that in some degree, the high priest acted rather like a general practitioner to the community. He was not being asked to comment upon the ministry received, but to confirm the healthy or otherwise status of his patient. We would do well to follow Jesus' example (Matthew 8:4; Luke 17:14).

The laying-on of hands – This ancient practice of prayer has become the focus of a lot of criticism, particularly in its capacity for abuse. In the case of the London Healing Mission or the Nine O'Clock Service in Sheffield, it has been connected with the alleged sexual abuse of the client. For many of the reports in the press, healing has in fact been identified with the laying on of hands. Of course, there is no necessity to lay hands upon anyone in order to pray for their healing. In fact, it might be positively counter-productive to do so. Should our client be a person who has already been physically or sexually abused, then touch for them is anything but a comforting reminder of the love of God. It requires us to be sensitive and empathetic in our approach to the other person, and to ask permission to lay hands upon them before praying.

The next important question is: 'where do we place our hands?' There are some teachers who say it is important to lay hands upon the troubled or affected part of the body for which prayer is being requested. This could be a dangerous road to take as the recent outrages have demonstrated. We should also be aware that to lay hands upon another is a power game of some sort, and if we are not careful, we could fall in love with the importance it gives us to pray for another. In the light of this, I am not sure whether there are any absolutely safe zones on which we can lay our hands with total impunity. Consequently, I suggest that when using the laying on of hands, we touch the shoulder of the person or perhaps their head.

The confusion of style with power – The healing ministry has long been practised in churches with an entirely different approach to prayer than the more popular charismatic models. They have tended to be quiet and sacramental in context and usually the prayers are quite short and there is no prayer counselling associated with it. However, this does not mean that they are any less effective in their desire to heal. We must be honest and acknowledge that many models for healing have been adopted because they suggest that there is more power around. Some are excited at the sight of people falling, laughing and generally responding to prayer in a definite physical way. It is assumed that this is God at work, and as a general comment, it is open to fault. This mistaken view is certainly true of how some churches have sought to incorporate the house-style of the Toronto Blessing and so change their format of prayer ministry. I sometimes think that only the brave or the bold would then come forward for ministry. The quieter and more reflective temperament is often marginalized in this process.

'In the service of Christ the Healer'

We have examined some of the inherently harmful effects of the Christian healing ministry and offered some suggestions as to how to avoid them. My objective in doing this is not to prevent but to practise this work of care, but within safe guidelines. With the public attention now aroused in the healing ministry following the scandals of sexual abuse, it is incumbent upon all of us to offer a safe and accountable form of healing ministry which is open to both Church and secular scrutiny. This should not surprise nor alarm us when we consider that the work of counselling has already gone down this road. I think the days are long gone when the Church thinks it can practise its ministry without being answerable for its standards, its failures and its effects upon others. Therefore, I would like to suggest a few factors which will enrich our practice and exploration of care and healing for others.

Firstly, as Christians we should be open and welcoming of the enabling power and presence of the Holy Spirit to teach and guide us into healing encounters. This means not being automatically dismissive of every style which does not suit our temperament. We should be warmly critical of the new as well as open to developing and broadening what we are all too familiar with.

Secondly, we should encourage ways of discerning what are good practices and principles of praying for others. To some degree, this material has already been explored by the more established healing societies. I sometimes detect an arrogance within the charismatic renewal which implies no need of advice or teaching from those outside its camp. We would do well to humble ourselves and learn from the more experienced, so that our ministry can be all the better for it.

Finally, we should keep in the forefront of our minds that healing is never an end in itself. It is not a consumerist ministry which panders to the wants and obsessions of others. It is a servant ministry which once received is to be given away as gift and good news to others. Consequently, we could do no better in our healing ministry than adopt the goal of William Temple, former Archbishop of Canterbury, who would settle for nothing less than to see 'the Church and nation renewed in the service of Christ the Healer.'

5

The Other Side of Joy
Harmful Religion in an Anabaptist Community
Julius H. Rubin

Contemporary social science and pastoral theology share a common understanding of religion as contributing to the personal well-being of the faithful. From this perspective, religion creates a symbolic system of meanings and ultimate values that offers comprehensive answers to the vexing questions of human existence: the meaning of life, the relationship of men and women to God, the problem of evil and suffering in the world, the nature of ethical conduct, and the promise of salvation or one's fate after death. Religious affiliation offers membership into integrated groups, collective identifications that support individual identity, and participation in emotionally satisfying cathartic rituals. The positive functions of religion include: reduction of existential anxiety, a sense of hope and well-being, a coherent ethos to guide conduct, social support in times of adversity, avoidance of self-destructive behaviour, and a purpose for life for believers assured of their relationship with a transcendental Other. Thus, religion promotes times of joyful communion with God and co-religionists.[1]

'High-demand' groups', 'strong churches' and world-rejecting sects limit their membership to the 'religiously qualified', enjoining them to shape their lives, identities, and daily conduct in conformity with God-willed ethical action. Believers immerse themselves in religion and mould their lives to serve religious ends. They eschew a compartmentalized, limited spiritual role of religion on Sundays or holidays in favour of a totalizing personal commitment to God. These groups foster 'church-communities' that integrate members into webs of social solidarity – brotherhoods of believers bound to one another in social communion and in communion with God. Here, religion protests and offers an alternative to the unresolved crises of modernity that have characterized the twentieth century:

1. Secularization, value pluralism, subjectivity and the problem of the meaninglessness of life.
2. The harsh, unbrotherly conditions of capitalist market economies troubled by inequalities of class, race, ethnicity or gender.
3. The coercion of the state and the dehumanizing rationalization and bureaucratization of modern life.

Religious affiliation offers the allure of authentic community, true family, and loving fraternity and sorority that contrasts with past disappointments that people encountered in worldly communities, families and social relationships.

American fundamentalism (1910-1930), European Christian student movements, religious socialists and evangelicals following World War I, and new religious movements that emerged during the recent counterculture, for example, have each protested the conditions and crises of modernity and proffered millenarian alternatives to alienation, anomie and existential angst. True believers here enjoy the benefits of their faith – a religiously-grounded self devoted to a calling surrendered in obedience to the will of God. They live a Christian life in concert with others that instils ultimate meaning, purpose and clarity.[2]

What are the costs of this religious vocation? Among many evangelical, Pentecostal, fundamentalist and conservative Protestant sects, religion also demands that believers undergo suffering in the fulfilment of ultimate values. Theologies that encourage conversion as a pilgrimage of self-annihilation of the 'natural man', and a life-long inner warfare against indwelling sin, often instil immobilizing guilt, repressed anger, sexual repression and maladjustment, anxiety over salvation, and impediments to personal agency and self-determination among adherents. These costs of religious vocation represent the other side of joy.

The Bruderhof communities

In this chapter, we will examine the other side of joy for one fundamentalist Christian community of goods. The Bruderhof (also known in past times as the Society of Brothers or Hutterian Brethren), is a Christian intentional community founded in the 1920s in Germany by Eberhard Arnold. It is now entering its fourth generation, with eight settlements or 'hofs', and approximately 2,200 members in America and England. They support themselves by manufacturing quality children's toys under the trade name 'Community Playthings', and products for disabled people through Rifton Enterprises.

Visitors to the Bruderhof encounter a peculiar combination of a medieval village community and late twentieth-century technological sophistication that includes ultramodern telecommunications, Japanese manufacturing techniques, a community-owned Gulfstream jet, and extensive computerization. Hof life appears idyllic. Violent crime, illicit drug abuse, or economic and material concerns are largely absent from their lives. Premarital sexual activity is prohibited, and single parent families are largely unknown in the community. Divorce is not permitted. Thus, Bruderhof families are not disrupted by family patterns that characterize the wider society.

Many journalists, visitors and guests have extolled the virtues of this Christian community by writing uncritical accounts of the Bruderhof. Articles in national publications such as *Sojourners*, *Christian Century* and *The New York Times* have presented an idealized and sentimentalized portrait of the community.[3] Local newspapers in American communities adjacent to Bruderhof settlements print a seemingly endless series of human interest stories that, for example, portray blond and fair children weaving garlands of flowers in celebration of nature and the coming of spring. Sombre, bearded men in plain shirts, suspenders and trousers march in a 'peace witness' against nuclear war or the death penalty. Women with heads covered in polka-dot kerchiefs and attired in long, modest dresses go about their daily routine with heads bowed in humility. High-minded men and women unite in Christian community as seekers of God's Kingdom. This portrait of 'the joyful community', while true, is incomplete, for it neglects the other side of joy that we shall explore in this chapter.[4]

The ethical mandate of the Sermon on the Mount serves as the biblical foundation for Bruderhof settlements. Believers, surrendered into radical discipleship to Jesus, strive to overcome their sinful alienation from God through conversion and adult baptism. They emulate the apostolic Church by devoting themselves to the fulfilment of the Sermon on the Mount, espousing the principles of pacifism and non-resistance to evil. The brotherhood holds all things in common, rejecting the divisiveness caused by private property and the pursuit of worldly privilege and power. The faithful are bound together in unanimity of thought and belief and espouse an ethic of brotherly love.

In strict conformity to the teachings of Jesus, the community enforces purity of conduct, thought and intentionality in the hearts and minds of true believers. The Church community keeps close watch to ensure that members hold to their religious ethos, motivated by the leadings of the Holy Spirit. They practise the brotherly watch to purify themselves from sin. Their ethos strictly regulates all forms of conduct, belief, appearance, dress and demeanour, with particular emphasis upon the repression of premarital or extramarital sexual expression. Brothers and sisters are prohibited from gossip or idle chatter. Should differences or conflicts arise between members, they must go directly to the person or persons in question and strive to bring a peaceful and loving resolution of these differences or 'unpeace'. Church discipline requires public confession and repentance of sin, and exclusion of the errant sinner into the world. Only by fostering absolute unity, the Bruderhof maintains, can it collectively form a vessel to capture the Holy Spirit in childlike joy, humility and surrender to Jesus.

The first Bruderhof community at Sannerz, Germany, in 1921, began as a charismatic group devoted to Eberhard Arnold. This countercultural commune attracted educated, middle class youth from the student movement and German Christian Movement, who rejected the rationalized orders of modern society. The early members of the Bruderhof embraced an ethic of universal brotherhood, assured of the millennial advent of the Redeemer's Kingdom in their lifetime. The Bruderhof relocated in 1927 to Fulda, Germany, to the Rhön community.

In the period 1928-32, Arnold struggled to develop financial, organizational and doctrinal stability for his charismatic Church. He found the solution to the 'routinization of charisma' by adopting the religious orders and administrative blueprint of North American Hutterite communities. Arnold travelled to America, received ordination as a Hutterite minister, and affiliated his community with this Anabaptist conventicle.

Bruderhof members steadfastly refused to cooperate with the Nazis, to surrender their sons for compulsory military service, or to utter the oath of allegiance to the Nazi race-based salvation state. One year before Arnold's untimely death in 1935, they founded the Alm Bruderhof in neutral Liechtenstein and secreted draft-age men out of Germany. The Gestapo and SS closed the Rhön community in 1937, seizing the property and deporting the members. The Alm community relocated in England in 1939-41, until the British forced the relocation of German nationals. The Bruderhof could not find asylum in North America, but was permitted to migrate to the underdeveloped Chaco region of Paraguay. The Primavera, Paraguay, El Dorado and Uruguay hofs served as the centre of Bruderhof communitarianism until their closing in 1960. After World War II, new hofs were started in Germany and in England. The community spirit was then driven by an internationalist, pacifist and brotherhood witness – actively waging peace in the Cold War.

Heinrich (Heini) Arnold, Eberhard's middle child, championed the conservative counter-trend, and continually attempted to redirect the movement to revitalize his father's theological vision. He precipitated three community-wide crises in Primavera in 1941,

1942 and 1944. Each time, he suffered public humiliation and exclusion from the community. Arnold rehabilitated himself as a missionary to the United States in 1950. The success of his mission and fund-raising provided the grounds for his reinstatement as a Servant.

The critical turning point in the Bruderhof movement came in 1954 with the founding of the Woodcrest Hof in Rifton, New York. As Servant of the Word at Woodcrest, allied with enthusiastic American converts, Heini dissolved the Primavera and European brotherhoods, liquidated the community assets, and excluded several hundred baptized members during what is known as the Great Crisis of 1959-61. This story reads like a modern Greek tragedy, marked by the internecine struggles of Eberhard Arnold's sons, his widow, and the son-in-law Hans Zumpe over power and vision regarding the future direction of the Bruderhof movement. Hundreds of people were uprooted; many saw their lives shattered as they were rejected from the new brotherhood lists and made to forge new lives after decades of faithful service to the pioneering communities in Paraguay, Germany and England.

The Great Crisis became the watershed that transformed the Bruderhof. Heini revitalized the movement in separation from the world as an introversionist sect, emphasizing evangelical pietist conversion models and extreme emotional fervour and devotionalism. Merrill Mow writes a justification of the Great Crisis and the acts of extreme unbrotherliness committed against excluded members in his commemorative history:

On this earth there is always a spiritual struggle going on; the two atmospheres are always in conflict... There is a spirit in this world that wants to destroy the brotherly life based on love to Jesus, and that spirit wants to destroy it right now. Every one of us has the responsibility to seek that love through which we may live the first commandment 'to love God' and the second commandment 'to love the brothers.' Then the brotherly life can be lived, and this is what we seek together.[5]

'A dictatorship of the Holy Spirit'

The Bruderhof and Hutterites share the Anabaptist vision of a community of goods, pacifism, and separatism in a Church community to recreate the Kingdom of Christ in dynamic tension with the carnal kingdom of the world. They are organized as inclusive Church-communities, where the exercise of administrative and religious power is concentrated in the hands of Church leaders who interpret the Spirit and word of God. The spiritual and administrative leader of all colonies, the *Vorsteher*, or bishop, is inspired directly by the Holy Spirit to discern the meaning of God's mandate as this pertains to contemporary matters of colony administration, the arbitration of disputes, or determining the future direction of the congregation. Individual colonies are led by a 'servant of the word', a combination of preacher and chief executive officer, elected by the consensus of all baptized men. A council of five to seven 'witness brothers' serves as an administrative council to assist the servant of the word. Witness brothers include the community steward or controller, various work department foremen and elderly spiritual leaders.

The Bruderhof members have passed down control of their movement to Eberhard Arnold's son and grandson in hereditary succession of office. This traditionalism is legitimated as emanating from the will of God, whose divine order has also created a hierarchy of patriarchal relations between husband and wife, parent and child, and leader and follower. Authority patterns are believed to have originated with God; leaders serve as his instrument, providing spiritual and temporal rulership over the congregation. They also believe that God decreed an organic social order where men exercise authority over women, and parents over children.

The promises of salvation are inextricably tied to the surrender to God's will and the believer's submission to divinely-legitimated hierarchical authority. In this manner, the Bruderhof instils habits of unquestioning obedience to the authority of the witness brothers and the servant of the word.

Church discipline derives from the book of Matthew, enjoining brothers, motivated by love, to engage in fraternal correction and admonishment of the offending member, urging the offender to seek repentance, reform and return to good standing within the community. However, those persons whose ideas or individual consciences endanger doctrinal orthodoxy; those who stand against the leadership and threaten unity; those who cannot or will not repent and reform from sinful thoughts and conduct, must be punished. First offenders or members who commit minor infractions are prohibited from attending the *Gemeindestunde* (prayer circle). The 'small exclusion', or *Kleiner Ausschluss*, allows the offending member to remain in the community, but under extreme social ostracism. The 'great exclusion', or *Grosser Ausschluss*, involves expulsion from the community.

The threat of exclusion proves a powerful and dreaded method of social control in the Bruderhof. A brotherhood member's baptismal vow to the community takes precedence over any natural ties of blood to spouse, children or kin. Exclusion invariably disrupts families as those who remain must shun the offending brother, or watch helplessly as their loved one is forced to depart the community. The trauma of ostracism, exclusion, family disruption and shame is shared by the family, falling most heavily upon children. Paradoxically, the Bruderhof stresses joyful surrender and abiding love, yet imposes the most severe penalties of civic-religious 'death', mental suffering and unbrotherly rejection of the unrepentant sinner.

The members of the Bruderhof institutionalized, by their own account, 'a dictatorship of the Holy Spirit', and a system of religious totalism that requires the undivided loyalty of their members.[6] The concentration of spiritual and political power into an elite leadership group of servants, ever-obsessed with unity, has resulted in the continued and systematic abuse of Church discipline as a political device to expel members, who because of individual conscience, question or oppose community policy. Such persons stand charged with sins of pride, selfishness and egoism, and are said to be motivated by 'the wrong spirit', or to have luke-warm zeal. The abuse of Church discipline as a political tool to stifle dissent or to redirect the movement, as in the periodic crises and purges, most notably the Great Crisis, has marked Bruderhof history.

Bruderhof teachings manifest an ambivalence toward childhood, simultaneously perceiving children as sentimentalized, angelic creatures and as tools of Satan – points of entry for demonic attack. Leaders have been obsessed with issues of sexuality, simultaneously seeking to repress sexual impurity from this age of innocence, while projecting onto young children and adolescents accusations of homoeroticism, bestiality and adult heterosexual misconduct. As Eberhard Arnold explains:

Sexual impurity is the most dangerous poison of untruthfulness and deceit. It robs us of our freedom... Purity is the essence of love and, like trust, it is the secret of the life which is God himself. The life of God is love in purity and truth.

The deepest thing that we can ask of our children is that while they are still at the innocent age when they cannot distinguish between good and evil, the whole atmosphere in which they live may be filled by the Holy Spirit of purity and love. That must be our chief concern, otherwise we shall be guilty of a crime against the children.[7]

Many Bruderhof apostates recount childhoods marked by family disruptions when one or both parents were excluded. Children suffered beatings, administered by parents, as ordered by leaders, with the purpose of using physical discipline to 'win the children to the life'.[8] Others tell of times in childhood when adults conducted interrogations, known as 'clearances', to garner confessions of sexual sin and impurity. After clearances, children endured forced separation from their parents to repent of their sins.[9] All too frequently, elders have labelled rebellious, intellectually curious, creative and idiosyncratic children as fallen angels, possessed by an evil spirit.

Young women confront the issues of powerlessness and gender inequality in spiritual and temporal roles, and severe limits are placed upon their aspirations and participation in the community. Women especially bear the burdens of *Gelassenheit* – resignation and self-renunciation to the will of God, as enforced by the patriarchy.

Bruderhof identity and communal living rests upon a radical restructuring of identity associated with the experience of conversion and the annihilation of the sinful, proud self. Eberhard Arnold drew upon the tradition of the German evangelical pietist theology of assurance – the necessity of an intense, emotionally wrenching inner struggle (*Busskampf*), resulting in the ravishing, joyous psychological union with God, the inner-worldly mystical 'bride of the lamb'.[10] Each new being is marked by an existential reorientation, separate from the kingdom of Satan and the world, engaged in a battle to build the kingdom of God. The new creation adopts the five distinguishing marks of the life of faith:

1. Trials (*Anfechtungen*)
2. Cross-bearing
3. Obedience to God's law
4. Trust in God
5. Joy

Finally, the life of faith demands an absolute faith in God, manifested by a child-like spirit. Daily life becomes a witness to joy in life and God – almost a literal song sung by brethren united.

The life of faith is not easily won. Bruderhof theology appropriates the Lutheran concept of Christocentric faith – the imitation of Christ's cross-bearing and redemptive suffering. Heini Arnold frequently directed his followers to Bonhoeffer's work, *The Cost of Discipleship*, rejecting the 'cheap' and freely-proffered institutional grace and salvation of the churches. Disciples who emulate Jesus, who devote their lives completely to the teachings of the Sermon on the Mount, are destined to suffer. As Bonhoeffer said, 'Suffering, then, is the badge of true discipleship.'[11] Thus, the life of faith alternates between joyful surrender to Jesus – the rapture of assurance as a child of God, fulfilled by his love – and the seasons of abject suffering – cross-bearing, self-accusations of sinfulness, and religious despair.

According to Bruderhof belief, the Devil looks to make inroads into the community by attacking the spiritually weak brethren, the emotionally unstable members, those who are tempted by the sins of the flesh, and those haunted by obsessive guilt, blasphemous thoughts and religious melancholy. Each believer faces the ever-present danger of demonic possession. The community confronts the perils of mammonism from without and disunity and Satan-haunted sinners from within.

In his book, *Freedom From Sinful Thoughts, Christ Alone Breaks the Curse*, Heini Arnold taught the brotherhood that 'there is no doubt that the Devil tries by every means to suggest to us human beings proud, evil, impure, even blasphemous feelings, ideas or thoughts – even the urge to commit suicide or murder.'[12] Only a Christ-centred psychology and a religiously-grounded personality founded upon evangelical pietist principles can cure the curse of obsessional thoughts and actions. The power of Christ alone can break Satan's hold and release frail men and women from the hypnotic power of auto-suggestion, where the mere thought or temptation to evil produces the compulsion to commit the evil act. The sick in spirit must surrender to Christ, bear the cross, purify their hearts and minds, and separate from the kingdom of sin to cleave unto the Kingdom of God – to the Bruderhof Church-community.

Following the founder's example of an exorcism in 1935, Heini Arnold fought the prince of darkness who had entered the Woodcrest Bruderhof in 1959, through the possession of a young novice, Miriam Way. This episode lasted from 1959-61, and resulted in her psychiatric institutionalization and ultimate expulsion from the community. The struggle for the soul of Miriam Way became the metaphor for the collective renewal of the Bruderhof movement.

'Even though the battle for this one person did not seem to end in a full redemption for her personality, it began a breakthrough in our Bruderhof struggle for renewal in a return to Christ as Center.'[13]

Arnold came to recognize the prevalence of spiritual sickness, 'cramped wills' and obsessive sinful thoughts and temptations among those youths and adults who struggled ceaselessly to embrace pietistic conversion. He explains why he wrote *Freedom From Sinful Thoughts*: 'I have put this book together because there are some in our households and even some who grew up in the communities who are really tormented against their will by evil thoughts, images or ideas.'[14]

Religious despair, suicidal inclinations and obsessions with unpardonable sin afflict many Bruderhof youth. Coming of age brings with it protracted and unresolved spiritual crises of conversion. Heini, as a servant of the word, provided spiritual direction for troubled souls, prescribing the practice of daily devotional piety, which consisted of prayer, meditation, and reading from Eberhard Arnold's writings. He advised sick souls to learn the technique of 'inner detachment' – silencing the ego so that the heart may open to receive the Spirit and love of God. When pastoral care failed to cure these spiritual sicknesses, Bruderhof elders turned in desperation to psychiatry, with the regimen of major tranquillisers, electro-convulsive shock therapy, and institutionalization of the most severe cases.

Faith: a Bruderhof case-study

In 1989, Ramón Sender, an excluded novice who had left his wife and young daughter in Woodcrest in 1957, discovered by chance that his child, now an adult, had died. The community had for decades denied him the right to visit, telephone or correspond with his daughter. He learned of her death a month after the funeral. Sender wished to learn more about the daughter whom he was prevented from knowing, and to write a book to commemorate her life. Bruderhof leaders refused to cooperate, so Sender turned to

Bruderhof apostates living in San Francisco, who put him in contact with other apostates. Soon, the ex-members began corresponding with one another in a round-robin letter which Sender and a small editorial group instituted as a monthly newsletter, KIT (Keep In Touch). As Sender explains:

> The KIT newsletter started as a modest two-sheet page sent to thirty or so names, but within four months it expanded to ten-thousand word issues mailed every month to over one hundred addresses. As the volume of incoming mail grew, four Bruderhof graduates and survivors formed a newsletter staff. By 1990, the newsletter grew to 20,000 words per issue and was mailed to over 450 addresses. Most of the copy consisted of letters received from ex-Bruderhofers scattered all over the world.[15]

KIT, now operating under the umbrella of the Peregrine Foundation, sponsors annual reunions at the Friendly Crossways Youth Hostel in Littleton, Massachusetts, the site of an earlier Bruderhof search for asylum in America. In 1993, KIT added a summer reunion in England (and later Germany) for European ex-members. KIT also publishes book-length memoirs of apostates under the imprint of the Carrier Pigeon Press.

KIT folk whose letters are printed in the newsletter feel compelled to express their outrage at Bruderhof orthodoxy, and to retell the story of the Great Crisis, having witnessed and remembered these traumatic events or more recent Bruderhof history. Many describe themselves as survivors, graduates and exiles, who are compelled to inform an indifferent world that the full truth about the Bruderhof must now be told. They talk about religious suicides and emotional breakdowns for so many troubled souls, allegations of the excessive physical discipline of children, and the ruthless repression of sexuality, as evidenced by clearings and interrogations of young children who were accused of sexual impurity. And many have brought allegations of the sexual molestation of girls and boys by adults in the community.

Bruderhof true believers and ex-members alike have suffered from the harsh, joyless aspects of the regime – exclusion and family disruption; the trauma of community crises, interrogations and clearances; sexual repression and the obsession with childhood innocence and sexuality; haunting fears of demonic attack; self-abnegation in the pursuit of conversion; self-denial of a woman's aspirations in conformity with the patriarchy; and immobilizing despair when judged by others as unworthy of membership. These themes are dramatically represented in the case of one Bruderhof girl, Faith.[16]

Faith was a child of the Bruderhof, coming of age in the late 1950s at the New Meadow Run Hof outside Pittsburgh. A vivacious, athletic, beautiful and bright high school student, she excelled and set her sights on college and medical school. Above all else, Faith wished to work as a physician in the Primavera Hospital and to devote her life to the Bruderhof movement. However, as she soon discovered, Bruderhof elders would quash these aspirations. Faith explains:

> The school sponsored a Parents' Open Evening. The brochure given to each parent that night reprinted an award-winning essay that I had written in my literature class. I was also listed as an honours student. Many Bruderhof parents attended and news of my accomplishments got back to the community which created undercurrents of disapproval. A Witness Brother met with the Principal and made it quite clear that the community would decide the right future for me.

The Witness Brother informed her that the brotherhood would decide her future and that she needed to submit to their collective spiritual wisdom. Faith replied, 'My only desire was to devote myself completely to the community, and I accepted this wholeheartedly'.

Faith read excerpts from a popular and forbidden novel, *The Catcher in the Rye*, and shared her find with another high-schooler, Hope, the daughter of a servant of the word. She recounts the interrogations, clearings, and draconian Church discipline that followed the discovery of her sin.

After graduation Hope confessed to her father that both she and I had read and shared erotic excerpts from *The Catcher in the Rye*. I was summoned to speak with the Witness Brother and immediately confessed my sin, admitting that I felt defiled and ashamed by my actions.

He asked me to describe this forbidden material, but I was too embarrassed to comply. He asked intimate questions and accused me of having improper motives for wanting to become a doctor. He continued his interrogation by asking specific questions about the plot of *The Catcher in the Rye*, about many episodes that I had not even read. He asked sexually explicit questions using words that I had never heard before. (Later, when I looked up these words in a dictionary, I didn't think that I could look this man in the eyes again.)

This interrogation was horrible and proved more sexually revealing than the few paragraphs I read from the novel. I made a confession of personal sin which was to be used repeatedly against me in future interrogations as evidence of my depravity.

Faith was prevented from entering a baptism preparation group, from proceeding with college, or from working in the baby house or with children. She joined the cleaning crew and later endured months of social ostracism and the small exclusion at another hof. Another servant of the word continued the clearance, probing for more evidence of eroticism and sexual sin. Faith explains:

He asked me to open up and confess about wrong relationships as others, unnamed, had confessed to impure feelings about me. He always spoke in such nebulous language. I admitted that I had sat next to a boy on the coach trip back from summer camp. We had talked quite a bit and then dozed, leaning against each other. I liked the boy a lot and fantasised that one day we might be married. (I learned that he too had been interrogated after my confession. He ran away from Oak Lake. I felt absolutely dreadful. It seemed to be my fault.)

I sank deeper and deeper into despair. I could barely sleep or eat or speak. It was decided that I was to spend some time away. I was petrified. I was taken to a cheap hotel next to the railroad. All night long, loud, raucous voices filled the air. I was too frightened to step outside my room, even to go to the toilet or to find something to eat. The next day I went to the Social Security Office, where someone from the hof helped me sort out my papers and find work as a home-help caring for two young children. I spent two months in this outside family. I was somehow able to convince the Witness Brother in my letter and after his visit, that I had truly repented and was now able to renew my faith and commitment to Jesus and the community.

Several months later, she was invited to join Woodcrest, where Heini Arnold joined the interrogation. During a prayer meeting, she fainted, convinced that God had stricken down so great a sinner:

That night in the *Gemeindestunde*, someone suggested the song, *Now passed is the darkness, the night is overcome*. The despair and turmoil and now this song. It was just too much! Suddenly, the room darkened and I fainted. I found myself coming round in a lobby outside the meeting. Surely God had struck me down for my sins.

In the weeks that followed, Heini Arnold continued the clearances:

I sobbed and begged for forgiveness. I said I wished I were dead. Life held no future for anyone as wicked as me. He told me to kneel down and he prayed for me to be given the strength to open up and to be totally truthful. This was demeaning, frightening and unpleasant. I was overwhelmed by anxiety and felt a sick, churned up feeling in the pit of my stomach.

These sessions seemed to drag on interminably. There were such long silences between his utterances. I felt that I was drowning in the silence, gasping for breath, but unable to speak.

Faith entered a clinical depression and was treated by a Kingston psychiatrist, who prescribed major tranquillisers and sedatives. She became increasingly depersonalized and suicidal, but refused to submit to electro-convulsive shock therapy. Thus, after months of suffering from intractable depression, Arnold sent her, unaccompanied, to the Bruderhof in England. Here the interrogations continued by another servant and his wife. After one devastating round of clearances, Faith attempted suicide by taking an overdose of sedatives. The Bruderhof expelled her and she began her life as an apostate. She explains:

I sank into the 'Slough of Despond.' My situation seemed irretrievably hopeless. I wanted to die. I managed to swallow a bottle of liquid chloral hydrate sleeping medication that was kept near the wash-up sink. By morning my miserable existence would be at an end. I lay down on my bed, my body racked by sobbing. I had no moment of regret or uncertainty.

I came round hours later, retching uncontrollably, covered with my own vomit. My head was exploding and I was unable to move my body. My attempted suicide ended my life with the Bruderhof. They informed me that because I had rejected psychiatric help and had rejected their attempts to cleanse myself of sin through confession, then clearly I must leave and find my own way of reaching out to Jesus for help. Thus began my separation from and new life outside of the Bruderhof.

The Bruderhof, like other new religious movements, conservative Protestant churches, charismatic communities and Anabaptist groups (including the Hutterites, Mennonites and Amish), struggles with its radical vision of discipleship, Church unity, and separation from the world. Each group seeks to form and reform a primitive apostolic Church-community of the in-gathered faithful in fundamental conformity with their respective theological visions of God's plan for humanity. The Anabaptist vision has resulted in schism and bitter division, and for the Bruderhof, the abuse of the exclusion and Church discipline. Submission to the patriarchy for women, and self-annihilation for all believers, has demanded the sacrifice of autonomous individual identity and self-determination – a significant cost of religious vocation. Pietistic conversion, and the making of a Christian life through redemptive suffering, engender times of joyful surrender, together with religious travail and despair. In the pursuit of such sublime ideals, the faithful will know the other side of joy.[17]

6

Theology and Political Correctness

Alan J. Torrance

This chapter is the outcome of a request to address the topic of political correctness in an autobiographical way. Since 'political correctness' is an expression too often used pejoratively of a genuine concern for fairness and equality, and given my deep-seated suspicion of autobiographical discussions of theological issues, my initial reaction was to view the invitation with some hesitation.

However, there remains a plea in many theological contexts for forms of dialogue which are 'earthed' in human situations. Given this and the need to illustrate the dilemmas and inconsistencies raised by the struggle for justice, fairness and equality, the discussion opens with an account of events which took place in a particular theological college. My sole concern throughout, however, is to do as my title suggests, namely, to focus on the *theological* challenges and issues associated with political correctness.[1]

Political correctness and ideological tyranny

A particular week in March 1987 will remain engraved on my mind for the rest of my days. I had just uprooted myself with my wife and family, left my home in Scotland, together with a lectureship in my *alma mater*, and taken up the chair of theology in Knox Theological Hall, Dunedin, New Zealand – the theological college of the Presbyterian Church of Aotearoa-New Zealand. Still suffering from jet-lag and living out of a suitcase, I arrived at the Hall to give my first lecture. The room was packed with students, most of whom, I was to discover, did not belong to the class and had simply turned up to check out theological orientation.

When my lecture (which was on Christology) came to an end, I was promptly taken to task by indignant students. Was I not aware how damaging, alienating and oppressive my language was to women? In my naiveté I was initially puzzled, since I always used 'he or she' and 'humankind' and had regarded my approach as fairly progressive in this respect. However, the issue was soon clarified for me. Not only had I been linking God specifically with a male human being (what is known in the trade as 'christolatrous religion') but, in referring to God, I had been using male pronouns – 'he', 'him' and 'himself'. Feeling severely chastised, I returned to the quiet of my room and sat pondering the wisdom of our move to Dunedin – but also considering how one might respond to the challenge posed. Consequently, I knocked on the door of a senior colleague to ask him how he referred to God, what pronouns he used. His response turned out to be remarkably accurate: 'Well, I don't often refer to God in my lectures!'

Over the following five years, I came to learn a great deal about those causes which are too often simply dismissed under the category of 'political correctness'. On the one hand, I was made profoundly aware of the strengths of the feminist case and the case of those concerned to support the indigenous culture and people of the land – the fact that we cannot ignore the subliminal oppression and marginalization of people of certain groups and that language can and does function to condition people's perceptions and attitudes. At the same time, however, I also discovered the potential for ideological tyranny which can so easily attend and be served by a self-conscious occupation of the moral high ground. Furthermore, I also discovered how effectively duress and the gagging of opposition, in the name of such agendas, can serve the careers and the lust for power of its proponents.

In the Hall, lists were circulated of hymns which were allowable in chapel – hymns which avoided whatever language was deemed to be 'exclusive', not least, exclusive reference to God as Father. The ethos was such that if someone did not accommodate what was 'politic' either in chapel or in lectures, students would walk out, complaints would be laid and life would be made extremely difficult for those found guilty. To be tainted, let alone tarred, by the sexism brush meant becoming the ecclesial equivalent of a leper. In the case of students, this severely put at risk their careers in the Church and the acquisition of staff references and the support necessary if they were to be appointed to a church.

Another political concern related to the status of the indigenous people of the land, the Maori. As an active member of the anti-apartheid movement in Britain, and as one who believed in and advocated counter-discriminatory measures, I felt fairly confident that I was free of racist attitudes. But in terms of the ethos of the Theological Hall, it turned out that liberation in this area went rather further than I had anticipated. To affirm the Maori (and not to betray one's status as in-comer and guest within their land) meant endorsing and affirming unambiguously the forms of spirituality which constituted their identity and all that went with it. To suggest, even subliminally, that God's work in Christ bore decisive importance for who we are was assumed to be subversive of the dignity of the people of the land, of the value of their truth-claims. It was deemed spiritually arrogant and designed to perpetuate western or European ideological supremacy. In sum, to affirm any specific theological significance attaching uniquely to Christ constituted a form of social offence akin to racism.

So when a senior professor stated in a sermon at a eucharist in the Theological Hall that he was sick of all this Jesus Christ 'crap', no one objected. And when he informed us that his Christ was the 'Aramoana Christ',[2] and when a hymn was written to this Aramoana Christ, this was greeted as indigenous New Zealand theology, liberating us from the oppressive colonialism of Eurocentric theologies oriented around a male saviour. The bitter irony of this emerged shortly afterwards, when a tragic, indeed evil, turn of events took place within the Aramoana settlement.[3]

The quest for a 'politically correct' New Zealand theology found expression in the argument of the first book published by the Faculty of Theology in the University of Otago. Its thesis was quite simple: the culture of Aotearoa-New Zealand is and should be the New Zealander's Christ – and it was quite simply inappropriate to identify the Christ exclusively with the Jesus of history.[4] The series of open university lectures which resulted in the book were vigorously applauded by a capacity attendance – many of whom were people who, in the words of a hymn sung at the Theological Hall, 'love the Christ and leave the church'.

These constituted two examples where the name 'Christ' (meaning 'anointed by God') was detached from Jesus and the Jewish conceptuality undergirding its meaning and attached to our own identities and cultural world-views – or indeed to whatever we chose to 'anoint' or divinize. Divine ratification could thus be attached to whatever ethical ideal, agenda, culture or place which we wanted to endorse either as individuals or as interest groups. The subliminal effect of this was not so much the 'christification' of our chosen object as the deification of ourselves – identifying our anointing with God's.

At the same time, there were acts of theological courage. After each of those lectures, a solitary undergraduate student courageously stood up (to the annoyance of many of those present, including his teachers) and asked the speaker whether, for example, he would have argued the same case in Germany in the thirties, or whether he would lecture in the same vein in the context of Afrikanerdom in South Africa. He asked whether there was any sense at all in which the Christian gospel might serve to critique or revise culture, and how this could be possible if it was our culture which was to be our Christ, and hence the determining control on all claims as to what was good, right, acceptable and our Christian duty.

In other words, political correctness came to mean radical, cultural conformity. The Moderator of the Maori Synod of the Presbyterian Church exemplified this when he came to speak on this subject to the entire body of staff and students in the Theological Hall. His dramatic address, which encouraged us to adopt and to act in accordance with the indigenous culture of New

Zealand, culminated in the following exhortation, announced with great conviction: 'As Jesus said, when in Rome do as the Romans do!' The puzzled expression on the face of the professor of New Testament was intensely amusing – the lack of any puzzlement on the faces of most of the student body was less so. Cupittean anti-realism was having its day!

The collapse of debate

If cultural correctness repudiated the Church's catholicity at one level, the feminist agenda, in direct parallel to this, threatened to do so at another. 'Woman Church' was established within the Theological Hall, involving eucharistic services for women with, I gather, exclusively feminist liturgies and diverse forms of spirituality. This was intended as a counterbalance to the majority of Christianity's resources, which in their view were irreducibly and irredeemably sexist – from its scriptures to its liturgies and hymns, and also its ethics.

The feminist movement of the time had strong views on the sacraments of the Church. One New Zealand feminist theologian, Cathy Wilson, argued in a book entitled *Women and the Church* that the use of water in baptism reflected the male desire to take over the birthing process, just as circumcision had resulted from the 'value-transfer' of the 'beautiful sign' of menstrual blood.[5] It was the concern of the male sex to transfer, by way of Christian rituals, the special value of women to men such that 'women are left without value'. 'This', she continued, 'clears the way for treating males as human and women as "other": alien.'[6]

In the case of the eucharist, not only were feminists concerned to reverse this process of value-transfer but also to remove the associations with violence which were represented in its symbolism. Cathy Wilson argued that these associations bear 'very close links with head hunting and cannibalism in many other patriarchal cultures'.[7] Such concerns were reflected in a painting on the theme of the Lord's Supper, which was commissioned by a group of women ministers in the Uniting Church in Australia. The painting, which hung for some time in North Paramatta Uniting Church College, shows a group of thirteen women (Jesus and the disciples) in ministerial garb, seated around a table on which we see a naked woman birthing her baby and with her blood flowing into a chalice. Around the side of the table is written: 'Take this cup... given for you.' Its message is simply and effectively communicated: communion concerns women birthing the spirituality that is immanent within them and feeding others with it. Women are their own, as also the world's, christs. The cross is 'domesticated', the violence removed and the supposed value-transfer reversed.

What is described above reflected, in part, the broader perception that the problems of the modern world can be traced to men and the toxic side-effects of testosterone. Male individualism and hierarchicalism were deemed to be responsible not only for war and violence, in their various forms, but for the rape of the world's resources, and the threat of ecological catastrophe that hangs over us all. Patriarchal religion serves, quite simply, to undergird this. The obvious conclusion of this line of thought was that women were to be the saviours of the world.

It was in this vein that my theological counterpart in Auckland, who at one point was solely responsible for all the teaching of theology in the Anglican and Methodist theological colleges, published an article entitled, 'Sisterstory: Women as Saviour'. There she argued: 'It is logical that women are the agents who can save the world', and it is women who realize 'the goal of a new heaven and earth'.[8] She then progressed beyond the traditional, Christian resources, and went on to cite Starhawk in advocating the inclusive, egalitarian religion of the goddess and the world-tree which she inhabits. The power politics of correctness was to find ever-clearer definition in a combination of feminism, pro-gay activism, post-Christian spirituality and nationalistic culturism. To endorse one of these elements was to endorse the agenda as a whole; to be shaky on any one of these was assumed to imply opposition to the package as a whole.

The momentum of those identifying with this agenda became unstoppable, and its effect in the context of theological education was devastating. Opposition was, in the nature of the case, self-condemning, in that it was interpreted as opposition to an inclusive, ethical agenda. What is more, dialogue and reasoned discussion became difficult. When a colleague who held radical views on the Bible was asked what she regarded as the critical controls on god-talk and on what basis the claims of disparate religious resources might be assessed, her reply was that this was a typically male question and as such not one that either concerned women or obliged them to answer. Not only was this kind of questioning rejected as male, but critical or analytical forms of thinking *per se* were explicitly and openly dismissed as 'male'.

However, the political correctness agenda produced its own 'intra-doctrinal' problems and dilemmas. Three examples bear mention:

Cultural correctness demanded that the academic year in the Theological Hall should open not with a Christian service, but rather with a Maori welcome ceremony, a *Powhiri*. This took place beside the Maori gate or archway, whose function was to keep evil spirits away from the Hall. This was said to be the appropriate way of acknowledging that we were guests in the land, and that our right to be what we are and do what we do was not the gospel, but the permission of the 'people of the land' (*Tangata Whenua*). For the purposes of the ceremony, the Theological Hall became a Maori meeting-house to which representatives of the local Maori tribe were invited. The consequence of this, however, was that no women were allowed to speak, because protocol forbids them from speaking at welcome ceremonies – indeed, women are forbidden from speaking at all in most Maori meeting-houses. This meant that the principal of the Hall was not allowed to speak, not even to welcome new and returning students. Neither were any of the women ordinands allowed to speak.

This gave rise to extended, fraught debates. When it was argued that the Church, as the body of the One in whom there is neither male nor female, must not be dictated to by any culture and must insist that the women of the community – not least our principal – must not be gagged on this important occasion, total confusion ensued. What was significant was the fragmentation and loss of orientation that emerged when the defining warrant for the existence of the Church was lost. When Christ ceases to be the defining criterion of the Church's identity it loses its catholicity – and in losing its catholicity it loses also its ability to speak to diverse cultural as well as to social and political contexts.

A second dilemma for those advocates of political correctness concerned attitudes to homosexuality. Most of the churches in New Zealand whose membership was largely composed of people of Pacific Islander origin were barely willing even to discuss, let alone countenance, the ordination of homosexuals. This clearly presented a problem for those committed to the political correctness agenda. Were the reasons of the Pacific Islanders cultural? If so, what right did people of European origin (*Palagis*) have to interfere or impose their ethical views on an indigenous Pacific culture? Again, cross-cultural dispute becomes not only unsolvable but unaddressable.

A further disturbing problem was raised with me by women from within the Pacific Island community. This concerned the extent of incest among their communities. They informed me that the patriarchal stratification of their communities, together with the associated taboos, meant that it was almost impossible to bring such issues into the public domain so that this serious underlying problem might be addressed. Here again, the cultural dimension of political correctness served to obstruct open discussion of these issues within the supposedly 'inclusive', Christian community of the Theological Hall.

In sum, participation within the Body of Christ became socially and ethically irrelevant in a whole host of different areas. Agendas and approaches were determined by extraneous and mutually incompatible criteria, voices and dictates. The extraordinary paradox of this was that in the name of political correctness, a new kind of privatized religion and culturally-conditioned spirituality began to emerge – precisely what those concerned with justice and fairness have opposed for so long in the West in the name of liberation!

It is not possible here to discuss the devastating effects of the ideological tyranny that emerged. Suffice it to say that it led to a reign of oppression and the blackening of candidates for staff appointments who were not fully 'on board' with the above agenda. I remember one staff meeting where a majority decision was reached that I should not be allowed to express my views (concerning the prospective appointment of a staff member to the Hall) to the relevant Church committee of which I was a member – even if asked. Following the staff meeting, a colleague took me aside and informed me that if I did not abide by this decision, life would be made so impossible for me that I would find it difficult to continue in the chair of theology.

The final result of continual attempts to fix appointments by dubious means was mass resignation from the Education for Ministry Committee,[9] leading to the appointment by the General Assembly of a semi-judicial commission of inquiry, convened by a judge. Most recently, a university review of the University of Otago's Faculty of Theology recommended that the operation be disbanded in its present form.[10] The Church-university concordat collapsed and the impressive academic and theological tradition of Knox Theological Hall, established over 120 years as a leading centre of theological education and research in Australasia, came to a tragic end. Space does not allow one even to begin to discuss the extent of the personal suffering of so many caught in the crossfire over recent years.

Learning the lessons

So what should one's reaction be in the face of the issues and events discussed above? The danger is that we use such an account simply to dismiss, scoff or warn against whatever might be identified with 'political correctness'. To react in that way would be the crudest means of endorsing other forms of political correctness. It would be to do precisely what the ideologues of political correctness do – to affirm and endorse uncritically the cultural demands of the context, environment and traditions within which we feel safe and which endorse our own interests. It would be to oppose one ideology from another ideological standpoint. For our purposes, three characteristics of an ideology require mention: an ideology serves vested interests; constitutes an interpretation of history, culture or the Bible in the service of vested interests; and is passionately believed by sincere people. Such a definition applies not only to the ideology of political correctness outlined above, it also describes the reactionary rejection of the concerns reflected in what is often too easily dismissed as the voice of political correctness.

To repudiate political correctness per se is to ignore the various forms of injustice and offence which fall within this category. The issue that should and must concern Christians remains precisely one of *correctness*. It is thus intrinsic to the theological task to ask in what ways we can indeed 'correct' and improve the subliminal assumptions, presuppositions and practices which condition and mould the societies, cultures and belief systems within which we live. Which of these stand to be critiqued and which of these stand to be endorsed and encouraged within the public domain? This is a question which should concern us all, not least those who despise political correctness from the perspective of their own agendas and definitions of political correctness – orientations, perceptions and apperceptions which often remain so deeply imbedded as to be almost inaccessible for the sake of 'objective' assessment and evaluation.

At the same time, the question must also be posed to those who choose to impose and luxuriate in easy solutions – occupying moral high-ground without serious engagement with the full theological, cultural and ethical ramifications of their positions. It is all too easy for one form of unself-critical conservatism to be replaced by another, equally unself-critical, neo-conservatism. In sum, the question which this chapter is concerned to raise is: how can we strive together for a true 'political correctness'? How can we strive for a true social, ecclesial, liberative and inclusive righteousness. And what is the contribution of the Christian faith to this process?

The first step must surely involve hearing the cry of those genuinely concerned for precisely this. To this end, we must now return to the concerns underlying the feminist movement within the Church. One cannot ignore the fact that much of the Church's talk about God, not least in its worship, is couched in 'male' terminology and imagery. Is it and can it be liberating and affirming for women if it is suggested either consciously or subliminally that God's purposes primarily involve men?

It can be argued that there is a male orientation and 'slanting' of the scriptural witness at different levels. First, it is apparent that the (Jewish) culture, which provides the cognitive and semantic context of the biblical writings, was patriarchal and that this is echoed in the text. Second, it can be argued that this led to an inherently selective (male-oriented) recording and rendering of events in the traditions from which the biblical material was compiled. And further, it appears that the editorial processes involved in producing the scriptures conditioned these accounts still further, in that those who collected and assembled the material accentuated the patriarchal slant of its message. There are examples of women who feature in early biblical accounts, whose place in the stories diminishes in favour of the male characters as the accounts are retold in later material. The contributions, for example, of Miriam in the Old Testament and Priscilla in the New Testament gradually lessen in favour of the accounts of Moses and Aquila. While there are other similar cases, we can assume that the fact that there are not still more examples of this is an expression of the fact that the majority of women have disappeared entirely from the historical process. The testimonies to their witness and contribution in the life of the Church are now, humanly speaking, lost in the sands of history.

That the editorial processes continued to downplay, or even eliminate, the role and contribution of women is reflected in the case of Junia. She was referred to by Paul as 'outstanding among the apostles', and had even gone to prison with him as a result of her witness (Romans 16:7). As late as the thirteenth century, she was to undergo a change of name and sex, becoming Junias (supposedly a male name – although not one that features anywhere else in ancient literature). As Bernadette Brooten points out, the argument in the minds of the translators was quite simple: 'Because a woman could not have been an apostle, the woman who is here called apostle could not have been a woman.'[11]

Not only do we have here an alarming expression of the supposition that anyone making this degree of contribution to the life of the Church could not possibly be a woman, but this distortion also served to compound this supposition still further within the Church throughout the following centuries. It eliminated a prime exemplar of the kind of role which women, as well as men, might be modelling. Cases of this kind confirm the extent to which accounts of past events tend to concern a history that is indeed 'his-story' rather than 'her-story', thereby ensuring that future history is likely to remain 'his-story'.

This highlights the important question as to the effect on role-modelling of the 'biblical' assumption that the contributions of women cannot be as worthy or as important as those of men. If the majority of the figures who feature prominently in the Christian scriptures are men, what is the effect of this on Christian communities? Is it not likely to lead to the assumption – either explicitly or, more dangerously perhaps, subliminally – that God uses men first and women only when a suitable man cannot be found? In other words, may not its effect over time be to seduce us into thinking that men have greater spiritual value or use than women, and therefore a greater contribution to make to the life of the Church? Indeed, has not the result been precisely such a view and have not quotations like 1 Timothy 2:11-15 been used to endorse it?

Clearly, a further important issue, which should be raised here, concerns the very way we refer to God in the life of the Church. The trinitarian formula uses terms of two persons of the Trinity which function at the human level to denote male persons. Further, much of the imagery that is used of God in liturgy is male, and God is traditionally referred to as 'he'. Any fair-minded person must surely be encouraged to ask whether this does not function (subliminally perhaps) in people's minds to suggest divine ratification of the assumed superiority of the male gender.

The subliminal influence of language on our thinking

Traditionally, it has been thought that we create pure concepts of things in our minds and then attach names to these. For example, we have a pure concept of God and then we attach terms like 'Father' to this. What matters is the concept and not the name. Consequently, if the concept is not exclusive, then the gender of the name is assumed to be irrelevant. However, recent philosophy, experimental psychology and educational theory have all shown that things are not quite so simple.

As philosophers have made clear for decades, language-use is a skill which we learn and it is as we acquire linguistic skills (subliminally, unconsciously) that we learn to make distinctions and engage conceptually with the world around us in a manner that is shaped by the language we are taught and the distinctions intrinsic to it. One might say, therefore, that to a substantial degree words form concepts and not vice-versa. People learn to use words and only then to think conceptually. Consequently, the words we use condition the way we think about reality.[12] It may well be argued, therefore, that if the words we use of God are all male words, then this may condition within us ways of thinking about God, ultimate reality and our value systems which are oriented toward the service of male interests.

This would seem to find support, for example, in research conducted by the department of psychology in the University of Otago. Elizabeth Wilson and Sik Hung Ng conducted experiments which suggested that even when general terms were used to refer to men and women, if masculine pronouns were used, people usually envisaged a male person. Consequently, when people heard the sentence, 'At university, a student can study whatever he wants', the majority pictured a male student.[13] In the light of this, Bergin, McKinlay and Mitchell argue that 'it seems fairly easy to deduce that when people hear, "in these last days, he has spoken to us", some kind of male God is imagined.'[14] In sum, if God is regularly referred to by the pronoun 'he', God will subliminally come to be conceived as being 'male' in some sense.[15]

If we think about the ultimate authority in male terms, it is suggested, we may find ourselves thinking in ways which endorse male authoritarian power structures. We may be seduced into adopting a patriarchal world-view to the detriment of community life, where people ought to be conceived as having equal value and status, and where people's roles should not be defined by their sex any more than by their race or culture.

A less subtle and more obvious area of concern relates, of course, to the Church's age-old definition of its structures with reference to the maleness of Christ, which has served to compound these problems still further. Not long ago, a Roman Catholic bishop emphasized on television that the fact that the Roman Church only ordains males is because it is integral to the priestly office that the priesthood 'image' Christ. What is suggested here is that if there is to be a representation of the one in whom there is neither Jew nor Gentile, male nor female,[16] it is absolutely necessary that his maleness must be imaged by the one who represents him. This immediately suggests, of course, that the femaleness of women can have no such representative value. Taken further, such an argument might be supposed to suggest that priests should also be Jewish by birth and retire in their mid-thirties! Indeed, the argument is so bad, one finds oneself wondering whether the fact that it is used at all does not constitute further testimony to the extent of the subliminal influence of the other factors I have outlined above.

Theological responses to these issues

So how does the Christian respond to the various issues and concerns raised? The rest of this chapter will be devoted to considering four different possible reactions.

1. Negating the negatives – One response is the quasi-Marxist one. Women are free but everywhere they are in chains. So the answer is to negate the negatives and utilize power to enchain the chains. In this way, the original thesis is addressed by its antithesis, enabling us to progress to a resolution in synthesis (*Aneignung*).

The article to which I have referred above and which was written by three of my theological colleagues in Dunedin was subtitled, 'Turning the Male World Upside Down'. The thrust of the article was to facilitate, by antithetical opposition to traditional theological affirmations, a final synthesis in mysticism. 'We may be at a period in our Christian history when an "agnosticism" with regard to terms for God may be required. And then throughout the time of silence, the old traditional images and the old untraditional images, the tested and the new, will together be able to lead us further into the Mystery who is God.'[17]

Plausible though this approach may appear in the face of the problems outlined above, it raises problems of its own. It is difficult to perceive any justification for interpreting such an approach as a theological one at all as it is less than clear what the controls on its god-talk are conceived to be. Silence? The passage of time? A change of fashions? Some emerging unitary and cohesive perception? On what basis are we entitled to believe that there is a God who will speak through this silence and thus bring us to a *theological* resolution at all? Is this something we know in advance – and if so, on what grounds?

Moreover, given what is at least a superficial incompatibility between the view of God suggested here and the Church's self-definition as the Body of Christ, it is difficult to explain how this approach does not end up simply using the Church for post-

Christian ends. Indeed, one wonders whether there may not be greater integrity here in Marxism itself!

Putting theology to one side, however, this approach raises the question as to how we determine what are to be regarded as 'negatives', what precisely the nature of their negativity is, and what an appropriately 'positive' or constructive response might be. Social history suggests that negating the negatives can engender highly oppressive dynamics and regimes. Negating the negatives must be done in the service of clearly attainable and recognizable ethical goals. Otherwise, the negating process can be substantially less than negativity-neutral. In sum, neither good nor God can be assumed to emerge out of any such dialectical process by virtue of some inherent necessity.

A much more profound, cohesive and constructive response is demanded by the justice issues raised above. At the very least, the whole question of criteria and, in the Church, how God may be identified with certain ethical criteria and not others – and, if so, on what grounds – is left wide open. A basis immanent in our self-understanding or experience cannot be regarded as sufficient since *precisely* such a basis or warrant will be claimed by all parties involved.

2. The 'pluralist' and 'inclusivist' responses – Another, apparently less radical, response takes the form of a positive attempt to be inclusive with respect to the distinctive positions of others. This is to acknowledge the existence of God, but to reject all forms of religious exclusivism (approaches which make truth-claims which are exclusive of other positions) in favour of a 'pluralist' or 'inclusivist' approach.

Pluralism suggests that all religions and philosophies contain elements of truth and true revelations, but that no religion can 'claim final and definitive truth'.[18] This leads to the conclusion that the main religious traditions share more or less equal degrees of validity. The appeal of this position is that it appears to render respect to diverse views and refuses to deny that those adherents of other philosophies and religions include among their adherents good, devout and compassionate people. 'Inclusivists' seek to embody both these positions simultaneously. They believe that there is one revelation or religion which is true, but that truth is found in various 'fragmentary and incomplete' forms within the claims of other religions.[19]

However, as Gavin D'Costa has recently argued, there is one devastating fact which those who hold these positions fail to take account of, namely, that 'pluralism must always logically be a form of exclusivism and that nothing called pluralism really exists'.[20] The obvious conclusion is that all so-called pluralists (and also, therefore, so-called inclusivists) are, as a matter of fact, 'anonymous exclusivists'.[21] Pluralism becomes logically impossible, therefore, due to the fact that this position itself excludes contrary positions – positions, that is, which it logically cannot include within its own position. All supposedly 'inclusive' theologies are seen to be as a matter of fact *exclusive* theologies. Consequently, the central question remains unresolved, namely: what is the critical control or criterion determining its truth-claims? In sum, this approach cannot succeed in addressing the central question any more inclusively than any other 'exclusivist' position.

Where a so-called inclusive approach is advocated as a politically correct and open religious philosophy, it is imperative that we see that this is nothing more than a myth – not an innocent or insignificant one, however, but a myth which deceives us about the facts and blocks our understanding of them.[22] The confusion here can only be seriously detrimental to open dialogue, whatever the subject under discussion. Pluralism and inclusivism, like the increasingly popular 'supermarket' approaches to theological education (where you are 'openly' encouraged to opt for whatever 'theology' suits you), all involve very specific, prior, theological suppositions which involve claims that are far from neutral. They are claims which are based on premises about whose nature we are being deceived.

3. The anti-realist alternative – Anti-realism or non-realism is the view that all truth is relative and that 'truth is the state of play' (Cupitt) and that the word denotes nothing more. If everyone believes x, then x is true. Alternatively, if you believe x, then x is true for you. This is the *reductio ad absurdum* of the inclusivist, pluralist agenda. It is no coincidence, therefore, that post-modernist feminism so often finds itself allied to this kind of position.[23]

The first thing that should be said about this kind of approach, which has been popularized by Don Cupitt, is that it can neither be stated nor advocated. To state or advocate it is parasitic on the ability to make truth-claims – which is precisely what the position itself denies to be possible. Indeed, the non-realist finds herself in a puzzling position if she advocates, as 'true', propositions which are not the 'state of play', since doing so must, by her own definition, be self-contradictory. To make 'true' statements, the non-realist can do no more than echo what is the 'state of play' and do so solely for the duration of the period in which the relevant affirmations are the 'state of play'.

At the same time, it is far from clear that this helps the cause of political correctness. If the patriarchy of the Old Testament conditioned the people of the time into regarding women as inferior – and, thereby, conditioned its women into oppressive forms of self-understanding – then there is absolutely no sense in which we can say that this was wrong or immoral. In fact, on the anti-realist account, the opposite must be claimed: the truth of the matter and that which can truly be claimed to be good and right, is nothing other than 'the state of play'.

If a particular ethnic group is hounded to extinction, leaving all those who remain believing they were morally virtuous in bringing this about, then it is true that they were morally virtuous in accomplishing this state of affairs. If Hitler had realized his vision and his propaganda machine had been effective, then it would have become 'true' and 'right' that the Jews, Gypsies and other marginalized minorities were inferior and ought to have been exterminated!

In sum, the feminist view that women should be liberated from self-deprecatory or detrimental attitudes is not served at all well by such an approach. The self-deprecation by women within a patriarchal society cannot in any sense be held to be wrong or inappropriate on the anti-realist account – it simply confirms the 'state of play' and thus the 'truth of the matter'!

4. Where does this leave Christian theology?[24] – The whole political correctness debate constitutes a dispute between two different kinds of non-conformity. On the one hand, we have its advocates who are determined not to conform to the oppressive conservatisms of our culture and Church. Its opponents are defenders of tradition, and are thus determined not to conform to the fashionable demands of political correctness. Repudiating the duress of its advocates, they refuse, therefore, even to contemplate meddling or tampering with the traditions, liturgies and resources of the Christian Church. So how does one adjudicate and determine which kind of non-conformity is appropriate and when? The issue obviously concerns what kind of control or criterion should condition or drive our ethical and theological decision-making and judgments.

Clearly, there is a false kind of conformity which simply conforms to this age – it allows whatever demands are in fashion to shape our theological affirmations. Its insistence, 'let the world write the agenda', usually translates, 'let the world write the answers'! The hopelessness of such an approach, with its ambiguities and unresolveable conflicts, has already been discussed. One could speak at length here about the dangers of 'Culture Protestantism'[25] and what happened when the German Christians advocated that our god-talk be shaped to meet the ends of indigenous culture and nationalistic agendas.[26]

On the other hand, however, we encounter that kind of non-conformity which ultimately becomes little more than the arrogant following of one's own uninformed inclinations, the dictates of one's biases and the uncritical perpetuation of one's own traditions, with no heed to the implications, consequences, damage or cost of these.

In sum, the political correctness debate becomes a dispute between two equally idolatrous ideologies in the name of divergent idealisms and value-systems.

A genuinely alternative approach, however, is advocated by the apostle Paul in his utilization of the concepts of 'form' (morphe) and 'world', in his distinction between conformity (literally, being 'schematized' by this world) and transformation (*meta-morph-osis*) which refers to the renewal of the minds of those who are true to Christ, that is, 'in Christ'. In Philippians chapter 2, Paul argues that Christ, being in the form (*morphe*) of God, came to the world taking the form (*morphe*) of a servant. The implication is that discipleship means that the Christian Church, the Body of Christ, should also be willing to take the form of a servant and to lose its life for the world, just as Christ went to the cross as the suffering servant in and through his radically inclusive love for the world.

What precisely is meant by this becomes clear in Romans 12:2, where the concept of 'form' is taken up again. Taking the form of a servant in the world does not mean that we should be 'schematized' by the secular world, or by 'this age',[27] but rather 'transformed' (*metamorphousthe*) by the renewal of our minds. Paul continues that it is then that we will be able to test and approve God's loving, affirming and inclusive purposes for the world. In other words, it is by this means alone, that we have access to genuinely theologically-informed, ethical criteria – namely, that as God loves the world so must we love each other. It is by being 'in Christ' and thereby having that mind which was in Christ Jesus (by being reconciled through him to God first, and therefore and in this way, being reconciled to the world) that we find *theological* warrant for a genuinely inclusive ethic. This warrant is found 'specifically' – that is, exclusively – and 'once and for all' in the concrete and inclusive presence of God with and for humanity in Christ, in the form of a servant – in the form of the one in whom there is neither Jew nor Gentile, black nor white, male nor female...

The authentic mission which lies at the heart of the Christian faith is not, therefore, to be conformed to or moulded by this world, but to be transformed and reformed for this alienated, confused, disparate and fragmented world. At the same time, real change of this kind commits the Church to a continual process of reform – *ecclesia semper reformanda!* This involves the transformation of our minds and of our theological speech-acts, so that we might share, by the Spirit, in the life of the one who was in the *morphe* of God and took the *morphe* of a servant. As this happens, we are enabled to witness to him effectively and inclusively in all our forms of life and in all our activities. The *metamorphosis* which this denotes has no place for conservatisms.

But does this not simply constitute an invitation to return to 'christolatrous' religion? Can such piety ever connect with the hard-hitting feminist debates about language for example? Let me end by referring to Matthew 23:8-12, in which Jesus himself anticipates and takes up precisely the feminist concerns about language.

In this passage, Jesus is radically concerned about oppressive and hierarchical forms of teaching that burden and oppress its subjects while serving vested interests. The Rabbis were securing and preserving their status by the exclusive appropriation of the language of authority – referring to themselves as 'rabbis' or 'teachers'. Jesus' response is simple and radical. This language is to be used of no one but the Christ. There is only one who may be called 'rabbi' and only one who may be called 'teacher'.

Moreover, Jesus does not stop with the language of 'teacher' or 'master', but also considers the language of fatherhood. Why does he do this? Because to use the same conceptuality simultaneously and univocally in both the human and the divine contexts functions to endorse patriarchalism and further undermine the egalitarianism he is advocating. Whereas contemporary feminism seeks to undermine the apparent divine endorsement of patriarchalism by opposing any subliminal linking of human fatherhood and divine fatherhood in our using the term 'Father' of God, Jesus addresses precisely this concern because of his emphasis on the inclusive egalitarianism of the kingdom of God. He does this, however, by taking a parallel and even more radical, alternative route. Instead of suggesting that we continue to use the term 'father' in the human context but cease using it of God, he argues that the term should be used exclusively of God and no longer of human beings. 'And do not call anyone on earth "father", for you have one Father and he is in heaven.' (Matthew 23:9). Consequently, we are all to regard ourselves as siblings – equal under God and related to each other in and through our heavenly Father.

In other words, we find that the concerns of Jesus are precisely those of the feminists. There is to be absolutely no utilization of language of God and humanity in such a way as to endorse human hierarchies and the associated forms of oppression. All hierarchical and non-egalitarian terminology must be reserved exclusively for God and the one known as 'the Christ'.

But does this mean that God is to be identified and understood in terms of a hierarchical terminology and the attendant associations with power or linear management? As the story continues, the answer to this question also becomes clear. Peter, we discover, thought that divine authority did and should function in precisely this way and was consequently incensed and angry when Jesus suggested that, as the Messiah, he must suffer. Jesus rebukes Peter, suggesting that his views are no less than demonic. He then goes on to redefine the whole content and significance of those terms he has reserved for God. He thereby redefines the whole nature and character of God's reign, as also the nature and role of the one for whom the words 'rabbi' and 'teacher' are reserved. Consequently, we find the true teacher, the true rabbi, taking the form of a servant and going to the cross – and in doing so, radically redefining the reign in love of the one who alone is to be called 'Father'. As Jürgen Moltmann has commented, the whole story of Christ takes the patriarchy out of fatherhood. The patriarchal traditions of the Old Testament are thus transformed in their fulfilment and fulfilled in their transformation. The prophet/teacher is the Word made flesh, dwelling among us as Immanuel. The king is the suffering servant.

The goal of political correctness, properly understood, is reformation and transformation for radically inclusive ends. It concerns that inclusive and affirmative social righteousness for which we are created. In the Church, it should never mean conformity to this world, to the conservatisms of any culture or tradition, nor can it mean the utilization of power or duress for the ends of any particular group. And neither *may* it, nor *should* it, nor *need* it, dismiss its christological grounds as christolatrous religion. For it is in the one who took the form of a servant – and in whom there is neither Jew nor Gentile, black nor white, male nor female – that we discover the most radically inclusive control on god-talk. And it is in him alone that we find theological warrant for a form of life which offers social and ecclesial righteousness, communion and liberation of a kind that is both more radical and more inclusive than anything that could be offered by the secular agendas of political correctness.

7

The Virgin Mary and Other Women

A Short Appraisal of the Situation in
Northern European Catholicism

Sarah Jane Boss

The claim that the cult of the Virgin Mary has been almost universally harmful to women seems to have become an article of faith in certain circles. And as with most articles of faith, its adherents have largely forgotten how it came to attain its current status, and have certainly not subjected their dogma to any critical scrutiny. In this chapter, therefore, I shall look at some examples of Marian devotion which could be viewed as 'harmful' to women, and describe the theology implicit in these practices.[1]

For contrast, I shall also take some examples of Marian devotion which could be viewed as 'helpful' to women, and describe the theology which seems to underlie these alternative manifestations of the Virgin's cult. I shall then suggest that there are non-religious factors which have influenced the relationship between Marian devotion and ordinary Christian women, and that, to at least a limited extent, it is these factors which have determined whether the Virgin Mary has helped or harmed other women.

The argument of the chapter is as follows: the changing relationship of the Virgin Mary to other Christian women is inseparably tied to the theology of creation. That is to say, the ways in which Mary can be said to harm or to help the women of any particular time and place is dependent upon how the women concerned, together with their neighbours, understand the relationship between God and the created world. This understanding is in turn closely associated with the extent to which human society controls its natural environment and the concomitant cultural construction of 'nature'.

Mary as harmful to women

Let us begin, then, by examining some of the ways in which the cult of the Virgin Mary may be held to have been detrimental to women's interests.

Cardinal Josef Ratzinger, in an extensive meditation on Mary, wrote the following words: 'The essence of woman was already defined in Eve: to be the complement that exists entirely in its derivation from the other, and nevertheless remains its complement. [In Mary] this essence reaches its acme...'[2]

So the essence of woman is to perform for man the flattering function of complementing him. Her existence reveals the nature of his manhood. Yet the converse does not hold. Since the man is prior to the woman, it is she who exists to complement him, and not he who exists to complement her. Nevertheless, the notion of complementarity might suggest that she is quite separate and distinct from him, and this in turn might raise the possibility that she could in principle become opposed to him. But this possibility is obviated by the fact that the woman's complementarity turns out to be nothing other than a derivative of the man's own self. The essence of woman-created-by-Ratzinger is apparently to reassure man of his maleness without ever having the power to threaten it. And with Mary, Ratzinger feels totally reassured and unthreatened on this score.

Now, we might reasonably consider that this pearl of the Grand Inquisitor's wisdom tells us much about the psychology of Josef Ratzinger, but nothing about the meaning of Marian devotion for women – or, indeed, for most men. Notwithstanding the fact that the Cardinal has progressively accrued to himself ever greater powers within the increasingly centralized bureaucracy of a global organization, we do need more evidence if we are to conclude that views of the sort that Ratzinger holds are in any way influential upon ordinary Catholics of either sex. Unfortunately, however, anthropological and sociological evidence of this kind is remarkably hard to come by: very few studies have been carried out which directly address the question of the effect of Marian devotion upon women.[3] So I proceed on the basis of severely restricted information.

The feminist theologian Mary Daly, in her book *Gyn/Ecology*,[4] contends that Mary is constructed so as to conform to the patriarchal ideal of womanhood: she is passive and compliant in the face of male demands – in this case, the demands of God – and she has been deprived of any autonomy or selfhood. This denial and destruction of womanhood, argues Daly, lies at the core of all patriarchal religion. Within Christianity, it reached its most atrocious heights in the witch-burnings of the sixteenth and seventeenth centuries, when women who were spinsters or widows, that is, women who were not under male authority, were especially vulnerable to charges of sorcery. Thus, Daly argues not that Marian devotion has been used in some direct manner to keep women down, but rather, that the figure of Mary forms part and parcel of a whole cultural system of misogyny.

Another, equally common, objection that modern writers raise against the cult of the Virgin is that it sets Mary up as an impossible ideal. She is both a virgin and a mother, which no ordinary woman can be. The journalist Karen Armstrong, writing of the Marian devotion of the high Middle Ages, says: 'As a role model the Virgin Mary is impossible. With the best will in the world no woman can imitate the Virgin Mary. She cannot be a mother and a virgin at the same time. To hear too much about these idealized Marys... could make [women] in the real world feel failures.'[5]

Moreover, the act of failing is itself tied to another figure in Christian mythology. For ever since the time of Justin Martyr, in the second century, Mary has been compared in various ways with Eve, the first woman,[6] and the comparison has not always reflected well upon the latter. As Christ was the second Adam, wrote the Church Fathers, so Mary was the second Eve. As Eve hearkened to the voice of the serpent, and brought sin into the world, so Mary hearkened to the Angel Gabriel and brought about the redemption of humanity and all creation. The intended function of this contrast is almost invariably to praise Mary, rather than to besmirch Eve. Eve's failing is the poetic foil for Mary's glory. Yet it can often seem as though this motif is dominated by a sub-text which states that Mary's goodness distinguishes her not only from Eve, but from all other women. For womankind in general becomes associated with Eve's wickedness, and most especially, with her temptation of Adam to do evil. Furthermore, this temptation to evil is epitomized in the sins of sexuality, which contrasts most strikingly with Mary's virginal modesty.[7] In *Beyond God the Father*, Mary Daly wrote, 'The inimitability of the Virgin-Mother model (literally understood) has left all women essentially identified with Eve.'[8]

In similar vein, the journalist Marina Warner's study of the cult of the Virgin takes the distinction between Mary and other women as its keynote. Indeed, the work is entitled *Alone of All her Sex*, a quotation from a poem to the Virgin by the fifth-century poet Sedulius: 'Alone among women you were pleasing to Christ'.[9]

None of these contemporary critics cites much in the way of firm evidence for the idea that Marian devotion has been harmful to women, although all of them clearly believe this to be the case in one degree or another. However, it must be noted that all three of the authors cited above come from Catholic backgrounds, and two of them, Marina Warner and Karen Armstrong, state explicitly that it is their personal experience which has given rise to their interest in their subject. It therefore seems reasonable to suppose that the views which they express are born of their own experiences as educated women in the Catholic Church in the twentieth century, and that the picture which they present of Marian devotion is representative of practices which they have encountered in the Church in which they have lived.

In fact, the view that Mary is a figure who is entirely passive and compliant is one which is articulated in the writings of modern women who are themselves devotees of the Virgin. Caryll Houselander, a popular Catholic author, wrote a number of meditations on Mary which were published during the 1940s. In her book, *The Reed of God*, whose most recent edition came out in 1991, Houselander invites the reader to contemplate Our Lady, stating: 'That virginal quality which... I call emptiness' is the beginning of such contemplation. 'It is like the hollow in the reed, the narrow riftless emptiness which can have only one destiny: to receive the piper's breath and to utter the song that is in his heart.'[10]

A similar concern with Mary's complete openness to the will of the Lord was expressed by the influential religious writer Adrienne von Speyr in her work, *Handmaid of the Lord*.[11] A key term in this book is the word 'assent'. This word signifies Mary's entire attitude to God throughout her life, and has its paradigm in her response to Gabriel's annunciation and her conception of Christ in her womb. Mary's assent is undergirded by her 'surrender' of everything to God, and her 'renunciation' of anything for herself. Both these terms are employed frequently.

It must be noted that both Houselander and von Speyr – and even Ratzinger in the quotation which I gave at the beginning of this chapter – are ostensibly concerned with matters other than gender. The complementarity, the emptiness, the surrender: these are all supposed to be the disposition of humanity in general before God. Moreover, the motif of domination in Marian devotion has not always taken even the symbolic form of female subjection to the male.

St. Louis de Montfort's popular work, *The True Devotion to the Blessed Virgin*,[12] encourages devotees to make themselves slaves of Mary. The book includes a prayer to the Virgin which includes the words: 'I give myself to you completely, to be your slave in perpetuity, keeping back nothing for myself, nor for anyone else.' This act of self-dedication is currently being encouraged by promoters of devotion to Our Lady of Medjugorje.

In spite of its being ostensibly different in character from the writings of Houselander or von Speyr, the logic of this practice is not fundamentally at variance with their meditations. For the devotee renders him- or herself a slave of Mary in order to become as humble and subservient as Mary herself, who is already a slave of God. In this way, the devotee comes to participate in the most perfect act of self-denial and surrender to the will of the Lord, which is supposed to be the proper attitude of all Christians. As the historian Eamon Duffy has written: 'Mary's receptivity and obedience to the work of God in Christ is not the model for some uniquely *feminine* mode of behaviour, but the pattern for *all* human and creaturely responsiveness to God, male as well as female.'[13] So the derivation of Eve from Adam is a type of the derivation of the Church from Christ, and openness and assent are the proper attitudes of every soul in its relationship with the Lord.

However, we should not be deceived by appearances; for these ideas are grounded in a particular theology of creation which is itself permeated by notions of gender.

An image of human emptiness and surrender

In the theology of Thomas Aquinas, the most influential of all theologians in the history of the Catholic Church, the relationship of God to creation is analogous to the relationship between male and female. In a rather prosaic following of St Paul's first letter to the Corinthians, Thomas states: 'God's image is found in man in a way in which it is not found in woman; for man is the beginning and end of woman, just as God is the beginning and end of all creation'.[14]

Furthermore, Thomas's account of the creation of the world by God is almost precisely paralleled by his understanding of human procreation. He argues that God created the world from prime matter (*materia prima*), which is entirely passive, and merely awaits the reception of form from the Creator, since, in Aquinas's words, 'matter in itself neither exists nor can be known'.[15] Correspondingly, Aquinas teaches that in human generation, the male partner provides the active seed, while the female partner provides the passive 'soil' in which the seed can grow. The female provides the 'formless matter of body' and the male provides the 'formative power' through which the matter receives its 'rational soul'.[16]

Likewise, the scholastic philosopher Roger Bacon wrote that matter is purely passive, and awaits the activity of God to realize its potential: 'The potentiality of matter truly is its craving for perfection, which, as Aristotle says, it loves as the female loves the male and as the ugly loves the beautiful'.[17] From this it is clear that the scholastic understanding of Creator and creation is partly articulated within a discourse of gender, in which the dyad Creator/creation corresponds to the dyad male/female respectively.

There is a good case to be put for saying that in the Middle Ages, the imagery of male and female was used in a very fluid manner, so that women were often attributed with masculine qualities and men with feminine ones. For example, Christ could be said to have nursing breasts, an abbot could describe himself as a mother, and Mary could be represented as a priest. Thus, the construction of the relationship between God and creation in terms of male and female need not have had much bearing on people's expectations of real men and women.

However, research in social history, and especially the history of medicine, suggests that between the seventeenth and the nineteenth centuries, notions of gender came to be applied with increasing rigidity to actual men and women, so that, by the mid-nineteenth century, men and women were regarded almost as species apart, with most attributes being unswervingly applied to either one sex or the other. Thus, the notion of *activity*, which has been so influential in determining Christian philosophy's understanding of God, came to be seen as an attribute overridingly characteristic of men, whilst its counterpart *passivity* became the almost exclusive property of women.

Against this background, then, it is reasonable to suggest that when modern Catholic authors present Mary as an image of human emptiness and surrender, they are implicitly drawing upon, and thereby reinforcing, cultural notions of what it is to be a man or a woman, respectively. Furthermore, they are attributing to God the qualities which are supposed to belong to human males, and thus hint that human males might somehow be more God-like than human females.

In this view, the Virgin Mary signifies 'female' creation in its proper relationship with the 'male' Creator. And for most of the created order – animal, vegetable and mineral – this 'proper' relationship is the only possible one. In the case of human beings, however, the situation is rather different. For men and women have free will, and thus have the possibility of rebelling against their subordination: of refusing to recognize the virtue of womanly surrender to manly assertiveness, or of the dutiful daughter obeying paternal authority. And hence, humanity becomes divided into two parts.

On the one hand, there are those who reject the will of God and disobey him. This first group is headed by the Devil, who is the original rebel and the leader of all wickedness. And on the other hand, there are those who are submissive to the divine will, and who will one day be numbered among the saints in Heaven. This second group finds its model and advocate in the Virgin Mary. Mary is therefore the greatest power against the Devil, and for this reason, she was for centuries presented as the unfailing opponent of heretics and infidels, and was also set up as the antithesis of Eve, through whom the Devil first gained a path into the human heart.

Mary as helpful to women

The anthropologist Timothy Mitchell, in his study of religion and society in Andalusia, suggests that the cult of the Virgin is always dependent upon fear of the Devil: that her *raison d'être* is to be a defence against evil powers.[18] This implies that Marian devotion is bound, perhaps necessarily, to a theology of creation of a kind similar to the one which I have just described. However, there is considerable evidence to contradict this view, as will be seen when we consider examples in which Mary could be viewed as being 'helpful' rather than 'harmful' to women.

We have already seen that modern, educated women sometimes regard the doctrine of Mary's virginal motherhood as something which implicitly devalues the experience of real women, who cannot be both virgins and mothers. The theologian Ute Ranke-Heinemann has even claimed that the doctrine of Mary's virginal childbearing robs Mary of her motherhood altogether.[19] Yet this feeling does not seem to have been women's universal experience.

At most times and in most places, childbearing has been and still is extremely dangerous. Women risk their health and their lives in giving birth to children. Now if a woman in labour is suffering torment, and feels her life to be at risk, then what supernatural figure could be of greater assistance to her than a compassionate and powerful woman who has herself given birth safely and painlessly? My research leads me to believe that for much of Christian history, a central attraction of the doctrine of Mary's virginal childbearing has been that it signifies an entirely harmless delivery, and that this has provided hope to women who are themselves to become mothers.

St Bridget, Queen of Sweden, was the mother of eight children, and amongst her many visions was one in which she witnessed the miraculous birth of Christ from his virgin mother.[20] After Bridget's death, the story of her life was recorded by two men who had been her confessors and had known her well, Prior Peter of Alvastra and Magister Peter of Skanninge, and they report that the Virgin Mary appeared in person to help Bridget during one of her confinements. They write:

Now at one time Lady Birgitta was imperilled during childbirth, and her life was despaired of. That night, the women who were present to watch over her were awake; and as they looked, a person dressed in white silk was seen to enter and stand before the bed and handle each one of Lady Birgitta's members as she lay there – to the fear of all the women who were present. When, however, that person had gone out, Lady Birgitta gave birth so easily that it was a thing of wonder and not to be doubted that the Blessed Virgin, who gave birth without pain, was that person who mitigated the labors, the pains, and the peril of her handmaid, just as that same Virgin afterwards told her in a vision...[21]

This association of the Virgin's safe delivery with the safe delivery of other women is by no means unique. At the village of Ranworth, in Norfolk, the Lady altar has behind it a group of late medieval paintings, including three of women saints with their children. These saints are Mary Salome, Mary Cleophas, and the Blessed Virgin, all of whom were safely delivered of their sons. When a woman in the fifteenth century came to be churched, or purified after childbirth, the dominant element in the liturgy was that of thanksgiving for the safe deliverance of the mother, and the woman would present herself and her baby before the Lady altar and offer a candle in thanksgiving for her safe delivery. The practice of women appealing to Mary for safe childbirth seems to have been very widespread in the Middle Ages, and has continued in some rural areas down to the present day.

Even in the British Isles in the twentieth century, Mary has been invoked as protectress of women in labour, as the folklorist Marian McNeill explains:

A charm still used in the Hebrides is the *Airne Mhoire* (literally, the Kidney of Mary), or the Virgin's Nut, on which the mark of a cross is faintly discernible. These seeds are carried across the Atlantic by the gulf stream and are occasionally cast up on the shore. Being rare, they are highly prized. In the Roman Catholic islands they are often blessed by the priest. The charm is used by women in childbed, the midwife placing it in the hand of the expectant mother, who clasps it tight in the belief that it will ease her pain and ensure a safe delivery.[22]

A friend of the present writer's, a Roman Catholic who lives in the Hebrides, has in her possession a Virgin's Nut on which a small silver cross has been mounted, and which has been blessed by a former bishop of the diocese. Late one evening in 1936, a young man arrived breathless at her door and begged her to lend him the nut. His wife was expecting a first child and was already in labour; a friend of his had lost his wife in similar circumstances and he was resolved to take no risks. The nut was safely returned with the news that all had gone well.[23]

McNeill also reports that the saint who is known in Ireland as Brigid and in Britain as Bride, is called in Western Scotland 'Bride of the Isles', and is said to have been midwife to the Virgin Mary. Bride of the Isles was formerly invoked by women in childbirth, which again suggests that there is a connection between beliefs about Mary's own child-bearing and the hope for a safe delivery for other women and their infants. These examples not only indicate that Mary has been quite widely associated with the protection of women in labour, but two of the instances clearly imply that belief in Mary's power of protection is intertwined with the belief that Mary's own labour was painless.

So Mary's virginal childbearing, far from separating her from other women, serves as a sign of hope to them. God's goodness to Mary is a sign of his good will towards others, so that they also can come to share in the benefits of his generosity.

Likewise, many of the popular medieval *Miracles of the Virgin* point not to any division between Mary and other men and women, but to the fact that all humanity has the capacity to be redeemed. One of the common miracle stories concerns a nun, the portress of her monastery, who falls in love with a man who comes to visit and then runs away with him. Unfortunately, after a short time he leaves her. She is then frightened to return to the cloister, and having no other means of support, becomes a prostitute.

After many years, she makes her way back to her old home, where, to her astonishment, she finds that no one has missed her. The Blessed Virgin then appears to her and tells the nun that she, Mary, has stood in for the portress, doing her job for the fifteen years that she has been gone, and that as a result of this, no one has noticed her absence. The nun is of course filled with gratitude, and she lives a devout and holy life ever after.[24]

The Virgin's sympathy for the lovers and the harlot stands in sharp contrast to the uncompromising condemnation of illicit sex which many modern writers associate with Marian devotion. Moreover, the clear message of the story is that even runaway nuns who are forced into prostitution are not outside God's mercy and are quite capable of being saved. The perfect salvation which is granted to Mary, therefore, is something which is to be extended to everyone. In these examples, Mary stands not for one aspect of creation, the 'good' side, in opposition to another, 'evil' side, but rather, she represents all humanity in its capacity for redemption. Moreover, she actually participates in the divine work of saving bodies and souls.

The theology implicit in these popular traditions is articulated explicitly by some of Christianity's greatest writers. St Anselm, for instance, says in a prayer to Mary:

O woman...
by you the elements are renewed, hell is redeemed...
even the fallen angels are restored to their place.
O woman full and overflowing with grace,
plenty flows from you
to make all creatures green again.
O virgin blessed and ever blessed,
whose blessing is upon all nature,
not only is the creature blessed by the Creator,
but the Creator is blessed by the creature too.[25]

Through Mary, all creation is saved. She co-operates with God, and everyone else – even the powers of Hell – benefits from her co-operation. Blessing now does not flow in just one direction, but passes between God and creation.

Mary as an active participant in the new creation

The notion that Mary signifies the salvation of the whole creation, and not just one part of it, has had a long history in Christian devotional writing. Maria d'Agreda, a Spanish nun of the seventeenth century, wrote one of the most popular works of Marian devotion in the history of western Christianity. The hierarchy have made repeated attempts to suppress it, but without success. The work is entitled *The Mystical City of God*, and is claimed to have been written from direct revelations of the Virgin. During the discourse concerning the Virgin Mary's conception, Maria draws a comparison between the formation of the Virgin in her mother's womb, and the creation of the world by God. According to Maria, the Virgin's body was created on a Sunday, and was prepared to receive its soul in seven days. Mary's soul was accordingly created on the Saturday following her conception.

Maria observes that this must have been a day of rest and paschal feasting, because it was the beginning of the work of redemption. She explains: 'During the other seven days preceding the vivification of the inanimate body, it was disposed and organized by the divine power, in order that this work might correspond with the account that Moses gives of the Creation of all things, comprising the formation of the whole world at its beginning.'

Although this account of the conception of the Virgin is unique, it nonetheless draws together a number of strands which can be found in many other Christian writings. In comparing the formation of Mary's body with the creation of the world, Maria d'Agreda implies that the stuff of which Mary's body was formed was analogous to the prime matter of creation, and this idea is one which seems to draw upon an earlier Christian tradition – that which sees Mary herself as analogous to the waters of creation in Genesis 1. In this image, Christ is seen as the new creation, and Mary as the matter from which that creation is made.

Several New Testament scholars have claimed that the Gospel writers themselves intended the conception of Jesus to be understood in the light of the biblical account of the creation of the world. Ethelbert Stauffer put forward this idea with regard to the Gospel of Matthew. He considered that Matthew saw the birth of Jesus as something that resulted from the operation of the same Spirit who brooded over the waters on the first day of creation. The birth of the Saviour is the new creation in which all things will be restored to their original condition.[26] The Italian Protestant Giovanni Miegge takes up this idea and suggests that in Luke's Annunciation narrative also there is 'an allusion... to the creator Spirit of the beginning, an allusion to the "power of the All Highest" that initiates our creation'.[27]

The American Catholic Raymond Brown likewise favours this understanding of Luke's intention. He points out that there is no Old Testament precedent for a virginal conception, and that it is 'more startling' than a conception in a woman who is barren (as were Sarah, Hannah and Elizabeth when they conceived their sons).[28] Because it is completely new, a virginal conception 'would be consonant with a theology of a new creation wherein God's Spirit, active in the first creation of life (Genesis 1:2), was active again'.[29] The Spirit which comes upon Mary is similar to the Spirit of God in Genesis 1:2: 'The earth was void and without form when that Spirit appeared; just so Mary's womb was a void... until through the Spirit God filled it with a child who was His Son'.[30]

The comparison of the Virgin at the Annunciation with the waters of chaos at the creation of the world is one which has appeared intermittently during the history of Christian mystical thought. Hildegard of Bingen (1098-1179), for example, wrote of Mary:

so you are that luminous matter
through which the same Word
breathed forth all virtues,
as in the primal matter
it brought forth all creatures.[31]

In similar vein, the twelfth-century theologian Rupert of Deutz wrote: 'The Holy Spirit, who in the beginning was borne over the waters, came upon the blessed Virgin and ineffably overshadowed her womb, like a bird warming an egg beneath with its longed-for brooding.'[32] The image of the Annunciation as a new creation is also familiar to Eastern Orthodox Christianity. In the West, however, the use of this motif fell into decline during the later Middle Ages and the modern period.

In the examples which I have given, Mary is more or less identified with the very foundations of the cosmos, and thus precedes the division of the world into angels and devils. Yet even among the authors just cited, it is interesting to note a difference of opinion on one matter. The modern commentators Miegge and Brown consider that Mary's correspondence to the waters of creation renders her entirely passive in her relationship with God at the Annunciation. She is inchoate matter upon whom God enacts his sovereign will. Yet the medieval authors Rupert and Hildegard, elsewhere in their writing, present Mary as an active participant or agent in salvation, through her accession to Gabriel's glad tidings.

The comparison of Mary with the waters of creation makes particularly clear the notion that Mary is a figure for the created world – indeed, the very matter of creation itself – in relation to the Creator. She signifies the matter of creation in the state of creation. This particular representative or symbolic function, I would argue, governs many aspects of the development of Mary's cult, including her relationship to other women.

We have now seen two different pictures of Mary's relationship to ordinary women, and two different theologies of creation underpinning this difference. In one, creation is passive and empty, as women are supposed to be in relation to men. In this understanding, Mary also is passive and empty. And human beings, and especially women, who do not accept this as their proper condition are in league with the Devil. In the alternative theology, on the other hand, Mary, a creature, actively participates in the Creator's work of salvation. As a result of this, all creation, without distinction, including childbearing women, wayward nuns and even fallen angels, can share in the joy of this redemption. What, then, are the factors which determine which of these theologies is dominant? That is to say, what are the factors which determine whether Marian devotion is predominantly harmful or helpful to Christian women?

I am obviously not able to attempt a comprehensive answer to this question in this chapter. But I will provide some pointers which I believe to be in the right direction.

Factors influencing Mary's relationship to other women

The way in which Christians construct the relationship between God and creation is governed to a considerable extent by humanity's own relationship to the physical world in which it participates. It depends on the use which is made of technology within the culture in which a given theology or devotion has its origins. During the first 800 years of Christianity, before there were great advances in technology, theologians, who were scholars, imagined God to have created the world through a purely intellectual endeavour. God contemplated the world into being. Then in the high Middle Ages, western Europe saw massive advances in engineering and architecture.

Lynn White Jr., the historian of technology, argues that these developments were dependent on a change in the technology of ploughing, that is, on the spread of the new, heavy plough in northern Europe from the eighth century onwards. Up until this time, the only plough which had been available was the light 'scratch' plough (*aratrum*), which was capable of tilling only light, sandy soils. For this reason, the only land which was put to agricultural use in northern Europe before the Middle Ages was on high ground with soil which is easily turned. The heavy plough, by contrast, could be used on the heavy, alluvial soils that are found on lower, damper ground. Since these soils are in fact more fertile than those which had formerly been worked, the new plough provided an immediate advantage over the old one for those farmers who lived in regions – most notably in the north of Europe – where the heavier soils are common. Most importantly, though, the new plough enabled the introduction of a three-field (rather than two-field) rotation of crops, and this massively enhanced productivity.

However, the use of the heavy plough required changes in the social organization of the communities which used it. The scratch plough had been drawn by only a single yoke of oxen, which would have been in the possession of the person or household who used them. The heavy plough, on the other hand, required several yokes to pull it, so a co-operative plough-team had to be created by peasants who had previously worked, in this specific regard, separately from one another. This entailed a complete re-arrangement of the system of land allocation.

Under the old system, the principle of allocation had been based on the notion that each household should have the land necessary to support it. Now, however, the combining of teams of oxen owned by different farmers necessitated a change away from farming which was centred on the household, and led instead to the introduction of the open-field system of strip farming, in which each strip was assigned to a particular peasant. Different peasants were able to make different sizes of contribution to their team (for example, some would own more oxen than others), and the distribution of strips of land to the farmers in a given team was proportionate to their respective contributions to the team.

The co-operative system which this method of ploughing generated formed the basis of the medieval manorial economy. But it did far more than this. As White has written of the transition from the household to the village economy, 'the standard of land distribution ceased to be the needs of a family and became the ability of a power engine to till the soil. No more fundamental modification in a man's relationship to his environment can be imagined: he ceased to be nature's child and became her exploiter.'[33]

A change in attitude of precisely this kind seems to be indicated by a change in illustrated calendars which began in the early part of the ninth century. The new three-field rotation was introduced in all the estates owned by Charlemagne, and a change in calendar illustration began to occur at this time, which was retained throughout the Middle Ages and Renaissance period. From Roman times until the ninth century, secular calendars were illustrated with personifications of the months, female figures, each holding her symbolic attributes. However, by the year 830 among the Franks, a calendar had appeared showing active scenes of ploughing, harvesting, wood chopping and pig slaughtering. The cycle of the seasons was thus depicted not in terms of natural or divine beneficence, but in terms of human action to make use of the natural environment. White comments: 'Man and nature are two things, and man is master. Technological aggression, rather than reverent coexistence, is now man's posture towards nature'.[34]

The new agriculture provided a greater quantity and variety of food than northern Europeans had ever known before, and this led to better nutrition and consequent improvements in health. The agricultural surplus also freed time and generated resources which could be put to new activities, including the expansion of the mercantile economy. And the perception of the non-human environment as an object of potentially increasing exploitation gave a new incentive to technological experiment.

However, all this was gained at the cost of enormous disruption in social organization. Villages were entirely reorganized, and the improved efficiency of the new agriculture, together with the increased population generated by better nutrition, meant that the proportion of the populace which was engaged in agriculture began to fall and the expansion of towns became possible. From the mid-tenth century onwards, new ways of life were established in city and country alike. Indeed, from southern Britain to the Rhineland, and southwards through Italy, the twelfth and thirteenth centuries were fairly obsessed with new technology, which was seen in agricultural, industrial and military applications, as well as in building projects such as the great Gothic cathedrals of northern France.

Occasionally during this period, God also was represented as having created the world in the manner of an architect or builder. The best-known example of this is probably the thirteenth-century French manuscript which shows God separating the waters of creation with a pair of dividers. Significantly, the image of God as builder was not used in eastern Christianity, where the technological developments of the West never found favour. In similar fashion, the seventeenth- and eighteenth-century Deist image, of a God who sets the world running and then leaves it to its own devices, is one which seems to emerge out of a human culture which was increasingly interested by the possibilities of science, technology and large-scale mechanical production.

So the relationship of God to creation is often constructed after the model of humanity's relationship to the natural world. We have already seen that the relationship of God to creation is also frequently perceived as a relationship between male and female respectively. In addition to this, we can note that studies in the history of medicine, physics and technology all indicate that the relationship between the scientist or engineer and the physical world which 'he' investigates has frequently been understood in terms of a supposedly male mind unveiling and manipulating a female nature.

Carolyn Merchant's study, *The Death of Nature*,[35] charts attitudes towards the natural world at the time of the scientific revolution of the seventeenth century. Her work indicates that there was a movement away from regarding the earth as a bountiful mother who should be treated with gratitude and respect, and towards regarding the earth as an object of rape and pillage. Opposition to mining, for example, was supported by two different kinds of argument. The first of these, found in Pliny's *Natural History*, and in other ancient and medieval sources, regards the earth as a generous giver of vegetation whom it is ungracious and improper to assault.

But this reverential attitude was not universal, and by the time of Edmund Spenser and John Donne, a more common view, and one expressed by both these writers, regarded avarice for precious metals as being equivalent to lust for women, and hence as base and degrading. In these texts, the earth is still female, but is wickedly tempting, rather than bountiful.

However, the protagonists in favour of scientific and technological development of this kind did not generally oppose the comparison of technology to sensual desire. On the contrary, they themselves came to speak of science and technology in terms of sexual advances towards a female nature. But this was not necessarily because they regarded nature as a delightful mistress. Rather, she was sometimes viewed as the potential object of sadistic assaults, whose secrets were to be extracted by means of torture.

What we thus see is a transition from viewing nature, or aspects of the physical world, as a female subject and an object of reverence, to seeing nature instead as a female object of male domination. Moreover, the tendency towards a gendered polarization of the attributes of the scientist and 'his' object of enquiry, at least within medical science and physics, seems to have continued down to the present day. As God governs the universe, so man is supposed to govern woman, and so the physicist hopes to penetrate nature and the technologist to control 'her'. This discourse of gender is given concrete form in Christian theology and devotion, in those instances in which the Virgin Mary becomes the representative of the created world in its relationship to a Creator who is endowed with the attributes of cultural masculinity.

Mary mirroring cultural ideals

In a society characterized by a low level of technological development, the physical world itself appears to be enormously powerful. Indeed, it is often seen as the bearer of supernatural forces, rather as the Mother of Christ is the bearer of God incarnate. And so it is that Christian writers of the earlier Middle Ages frequently invoke the grandeur of the natural world in reflections upon the greatness of God. They present the Mother of God as a figure who inspires the most profound reverence, since the Creator of this magnificent cosmos was carried in her very body.

The first verse of the Latin hymn *Quem Terra Pontus Aethera* marvels at the fact that the God who created the earth, the seas and the skies, became incarnate in the enclosed space of the Virgin's womb.[36] This theme remained popular in Christian devotion until the end of the Middle Ages; witness the fifteenth-century English carol:

> There is no rose of such virtue
> As is the rose that bare Jesu,
> *Alleluia.*
> For in that rose contained was
> Heaven and earth in little space,
> *Res miranda.*

In the modern era, by contrast, obsessed as it is with the intellectual and mechanical conquest of natural forces, the acceptable image of nature is usually of a nature subdued and compliant to human will. Whether it is a beautiful photograph of the Earth taken from space, or the ugly television picture of men landing on the moon, the message is in one respect the same. It is that the members of a unique and highly eccentric human culture are hell-bent on dominating as much of the universe as possible. And as the supposedly masculine work of the scientist is used to exert an ever-increasingly destructive domination over putatively feminine 'nature', we find that in modern Christianity, creation is correspondingly represented as the passive recipient of divine action, and the Virgin Mary is the very icon of emptiness and surrender. As humanity is to nature, so man is to woman, and so God is to creation. Creation is personified in Mary, and the representation of Mary therefore reveals cultural ideals concerning both woman and nature.

Even in the fifteenth century, at the beginnings of modernity, women of all social classes had access to a Mary who signified that

God's grace was available to them in all their necessities. Yet in the twentieth century, educated, urban women seem more likely to be offered something different: a Mary who lets them know that there are certain ways of being a woman which are acceptable to God, and others which are not, and that the cost of acceptability is one which is almost impossible to pay.[37]

In conclusion, then, I have argued that Marian devotion expresses several related trends within European culture. Specifically, the Christian representation of Mary expresses cultural notions of gender and nature. Whether the cult of the Virgin makes any independent contribution to this set of relationships is another question. But this is precisely the question whose answer is necessary if we are to know whether the cult of the Virgin makes any original contribution to the harming – or the helping – of other women.

8

Collective National Guilt

A Socio-Theological Critique
David Martin

───

'Crimes are committed by individuals. There is no such thing as collective guilt' (Lord Weidenfeld, *Newsnight*, BBC2, 18 November 1995).

It often happens that what claims to be Christian thinking is secular high-mindedness glossed by a Christian vocabulary. This is conspicuously the case with regard to the current move in the upper echelons of the mainstream churches to promote apologies between nations based on the notion of collective historical guilt. There are those who think that it would make sense and be politically helpful for representative national figures to come together, maybe in some holy place, and there express contrition and seek forgiveness for past historical wrongs. An example of this type of thinking is provided by Brian Frost's *The Politics of Peace* (1991). Mr Frost ran the 'Forgiveness and Politics Study Group' of the (then) British Council of Churches and is one of the activists promoting projects for international apologies.

I suspect that most people encountering such proposals would think them beneficent or at worst irrelevant. But even if they are merely irrelevant, I believe they trail moral implications that are offensive and represent a serious distortion of Christianity. I suggest that their use of a Christian vocabulary obscures conceptual borrowings from the presuppositions of nationalism. Of course, it comes as no surprise that Christianity can be partially fused with nationalism. What does come as a surprise in this case is that moves purportedly designed to attack nationalism should be so rooted in the opposing ideology.

Before going any further, I had better make clear what I am not arguing. I am certainly not arguing that religion is entirely an individual or private matter with no implications for politics and incapable of contributing to public debate. Nor am I for a moment suggesting that moral criteria have no relevance to international politics. After all, the Christian religion in particular turns around the victim who suffered violence in his confrontation with the *polis*. My contention is rather that the profound categories of classical Christianity have been rearranged and abused to subserve a version of secular high-mindedness dependent on a category – the nation – which is alien to Christianity. The subtlest heresies occur where one of the fundamental building blocks of theology is out of alignment. A misalignment at base undermines the integrity of the whole edifice.

Exploring the concept of collective guilt

I will put the core of my objections to these proposals, as follows. They involve an illegitimate transfer of the moral criteria which may properly govern face-to-face relations between an identifiable malefactor and an identifiable victim to the opaque realm of large-scale collective behaviour. Once this transfer is effected, the distinction between innocent and culpable is blurred. Of course, it often happens that culpability is blurred, but in this case it is blurred specifically by being attributed to every member of a social category. The category is the nation and I work out the argument below in those terms. But it can also be ethnicity, colour, gender or religion. The point is that the category, whatever it may be, is ascribed and involuntary.

This attribution to a social category not only blurs the distinction between innocent and culpable so essential to all justice, but implies the automatic transfer of guilt from one generation to another through membership in the nation, the ethnic group, or whatever.

It is therefore a grotesque abuse of the category of original sin, which is likewise involuntary but only in relation to the universal category of humanity. It therefore raises no issue of innocence over and against culpability. Certainly, original sin inheres in a collective membership, but it is a membership we all share in 'Adam'. It also passes automatically from generation to generation. But again, that passage across generations is not unjust, because it concerns the universal fracture of the divine image which we all inherit without exception.

The injustice and the moral outrage involved in the imputation of collective guilt through membership in ascribed categories and its transfer from generation to generation can be conveyed in dramatic illustration. If the ascribed category is nationality (i.e. citizenship), then the girl being born at this very moment in democratic Germany must shoulder responsibility for the deeds of some citizens of Nazi Germany over half a century ago. Equally, a black child born in a Bristol suburb of Afro-Caribbean parents cannot avoid acquiring responsibility for 'British' involvement in the slave trade. If that logic holds, then presumably a black child born in a West African tribe whose seventeenth or eighteenth century rulers sold their subjects to the slave traders also incurs guilt and responsibility.

I cannot believe that anybody can seriously contemplate such consequences without moral revulsion. But let us take the second and third of the instances just offered and see what would be required in order to evade them. With regard to the guilt and responsibility imputed to the black British boy in Bristol, it would have to be argued that he was exonerated on grounds of colour, whereas the white boy next door was culpable either on grounds of colour or else because he was genuinely part of British culture in a way the black boy was not. In my view, such evasions are just as morally intolerable as the original imputation of innocence and guilt in terms of citizenship. They should be repudiated.

With regard to the guilt and responsibility imputed to the black boy in the West African tribe, that conclusion could be evaded by showing that in West Africa there was no continuity of government or political unit or even territory over time. But what does such an evasion in turn imply? It could imply that the innocence or the guilt of populations depends on whether they have been so unlucky as to live in a social environment where territory and government have been stable and continuous. Alternatively, it might be argued that it is not populations as such which acquire guilt, but governments or ruling classes, which can be shown to have some kind of continuity with past governments or ruling classes. If the latter evasion is adopted, then some historical questions of a rare complexity are opened up.

For example, are the Howards of today, who provide an aristocratic leadership of the Catholic community, implicated on account of class affiliation in the deaths of the Catholic martyrs some few hundred years ago? Did John Major, as British Prime Minister and representative of a recent brand of populist neo-liberalism, incur the transferred guilt of (a) Lloyd George with respect to the Black and Tans, (b) the behaviour of the Anglo-Irish aristocracy in the eighteenth century, (c) James II at the battle of the Boyne, (d) Oliver Cromwell at Drogheda, and (e) the Norman-French aristocracy who set up the Pale in Ireland in the first place? If all this sounds absurd, it is no more so than what is suggested about corporate responsibility. If John Major should turn out to be tainted by Lloyd-George, the Welsh Liberal, but not by the Norman-French, one would certainly ask by what criteria continuity is or is not retained.

I interpolate a clarification. So far as I personally am concerned, I am perfectly free to judge a past action as morally wrong. Of course, I have to examine the complexities of the situation, the alternative courses realistically available, the likely consequences and costs of those alternatives, and the standards of the time. The same is true of a representative person such as the Queen. In principle, she may pass an adverse moral judgment on the land apportionment in New Zealand which followed the Treaty of Waitangi. She has, as it happens, expressed that judgment publicly, though it cannot be an act of contrition. Happily, some partial legal remedy is also available. But cases involving legal remedy are quite limited in number, because so few cases are clear-cut and the original contracting parties rapidly cease to be the only parties involved. As the case of Northern Ireland amply demonstrates, very little of history can be morally unwound without exacerbating the tally of injustice.[1]

In short, most of the expansions, plantations and migrations of the past cannot be undone. For one thing, all claims to be the original native population are themselves resting on previous migrations, displacements and expropriations. Furthermore, peoples mix and cannot be sorted out.

One has, therefore, to say that recent arrivals quite quickly acquire rights indistinguishable from previous generations of the native-born. They by no means stay in permanent moral discredit in relation to them. In practical terms, this means that nobody dreams of sending the descendants of the Aztecs back to northern Mexico in order to compensate the Toltecs, and nobody expects to repatriate all the inhabitants of North America back to their original countries, or the Irish Celts back to the Russian steppes. Any attempt to sort out sheep and goats in this way would, in fact, amount to racism.

Forgiveness between nations

How, then, does this bear on the question of forgiveness between nations? It bears on it because the moral accounting of some theologians really does depend on ideas of collective moral agency, based on an historically continuous corporation identified in terms of 'the nation'. However, my principal object is not to deconstruct 'the nation'. I need only to point out that the myth of romantic nationalism underpinning this concept of the nation was constructed by the efforts of poets, historians and political theorists, not much more than a century or two ago. The criteria of 'native' and of the proper boundary of the nation are all contentious.

Above all, the story of the nation in the national territory is a historiographical construction aimed as much at legitimating the present as at accurately rendering the past. What was a series of conquests and expropriations, one superimposed on another, is smoothed out in a continuing story of 'our' people, based on the contiguity of geography rather than the continuity of history. Kings Arthur, Alfred and William the Conqueror are opposed narratives welded into one. It makes as much and as little sense for me to claim continuity with Arthur as it does for contemporary Turks to claim – as they do – continuity with Homer and Herodotus because they lived in Asia Minor. All these narratives once deconstructed fall into ruin, and it is precisely such narratives that supply a premiss for a theological, moral accountancy based on collective guilt transferred over generations.

It is of course true that what 'we' call the nation does share intersecting cultural genealogies of a given character, which do over time build up and reflect a sense of common membership, and have come to constitute a group of recognizable psychological profiles. We consume these genealogies and absorb these profiles as part of our constant construction and reconstruction of ourselves as contrasted with others. This is how we recognize ourselves and others in the past, so that accounts of the British by Henry Adams and Henry James, and of the Americans by Fanny Trollope and Charles Dickens, retain some verisimilitude. We do inherit overlapping communities of memory, reinforced by the solidarities of common experience like war, even if these memories are rearranged and in part invented. And since our identities are built up in this way, we become creatures of the past, real and invented, as well as free agents facing on to the future.

Our pasts do flow along distinctive channels into our presents and it would not be unreasonable for us to be alert to untoward possibilities latent in our inheritances. But that does not involve retrospective responsibility or contrition, or place us either as nations or individuals on an international stock exchange of moral credits and debits. We are all equal before God in terms of his grace and our response to it. (So we might as well stick to the General Confession in the Book of Common Prayer.)

A major problem inherent in this whole controversy has more to do with how we use language than with ideology. We converse, we communicate publicly and we even write history in terms of loose, broad categories and collective nouns. We speak of the black experience and we speak of Britain's role in the Middle East, or British policy at Versailles. It is this use of broad categories and collective nouns which lends spurious plausibility to the kinds of proposal criticized here. Atrocities are not committed by the Bosnian Serbs. That is the way some Bosnian Serbs talk about what they call 'the atrocities committed by the Croats', and it is that social and linguistic premiss which leads to eternal feuding and indiscriminate revenge.

Such disastrous shorthands may or may not be linked to ideas of corporate responsibility, but they are retained in use because precision would be intolerably roundabout. Nevertheless, the result is that parts are regularly confused with wholes and individuals regularly taken to represent the character imputed to the whole. Moreover, it is the persistence of collective nouns over time which helps shore up the notion of continuous collective moral agency persisting over time. When a country like Rhodesia changes its name to Zimbabwe, we recognize the discontinuity. But when, like France, it does not, we fail to recognize a very similar discontinuity as if, for example, the government of General de Gaulle could be held responsible for Vichy and the government of General Pétain.

I offer an illustration from precisely the kind of historical wrong for which some theologians would demand expiation: the opium wars prosecuted by Britain and France against China in the mid-nineteenth century. A historian writing about these wars might refer to British policy and even say that Britain was responsible for certain acts.

But presumably in actual practice it was some section of the Foreign Office which thought there was an advantage to be gained by the opium wars, perhaps for the nation, more likely for some sectional commercial interest. In no way was the nation as such involved, and no blame can conceivably be attached to anyone now living. Nor can we reasonably expect contemporary British governments to shoulder blame for this slice of history, let alone express regret to the present Chinese government and/or people. The malefactors and sufferers are all dead and no legal remedy is available such as is available through the revision of the Treaty of Waitangi.

The principle is clear: those who did not perpetrate a wrong cannot express contrition to those who have suffered no wrong, and that holds whether we are talking of British citizens or British government. And if, incidentally, guilt were supposed to inhere in British citizenship, one might ask whether the Irish evaded the obloquy when they left the United Kingdom, leaving blame on the shoulders of the other three nations, including of course, Chinese migrants. As for those Britons who have Irish grandparents born in the Republic, their moral status defies imagination.

Two illustrations

That completes the exposition and I now offer a couple of illustrations which I use to generate some reinforcing comment. One is drawn from liturgy to show how political prayers can trail unacceptable implications, and the other is drawn from an article by the theologian Paul Oestreicher to draw out the looseness of this kind of political rhetoric.

The liturgical illustration concerns the prayers used at a session of Christian leaders in the North of England, chaired by Anglican and Roman Catholic dignitaries. These prayers were in a three-part sequence, the first invoking ecclesiastical genealogies: 'We are the Children of Rome, Canterbury, etc.'; the second invoking cultural 'credits': 'We are the Children of Bach, Beethoven, Chopin, etc.'; the third invoking cultural stains – 'We are the Children of Auschwitz, etc.'. After this third prayer, we were asked to say *Kyrie eleison* ('Lord have mercy upon us'), clearly implying that 'we', in some pan-

European sense, bore a responsibility with regard to such crimes, for which we might properly ask God's mercy.

Clearly, the problem begins with the second item in the sequence, where we assembled 'our' cultural credits or genealogies or whatever else it was we were informing God about. The strong impression given is that these prayers balanced credits against debits, sources of pride against reasons for shame. It is of course true that Bach, Beethoven and Chopin are in a general way part of European culture, but do I as an Englishman and member of the EC give thanks for them? Is an Israeli, or a Japanese, or a Pennsylvania German excluded from giving thanks for them? Supposing we had declared ourselves 'children of Shakespeare'. Would I, as an Englishman, offer special thanks by comparison with an American, an Indian or a Caribbean – or indeed anybody anywhere? Clearly, the implications of cultural self-accreditation in terms of national or European citizenship are distinctly odd.

That being so, is it not even odder to express contrition for Auschwitz in terms of European citizenship, or some entity such as 'Christian Europe'? All kinds of questions spring to mind. Should 'we' be contrite about the Katyn massacre, which though it took place on European soil was perpetrated by Russians? Are American and Caribbean Christians excluded from responsibility for what happens in (so-called) Christian Europe? It so happened that a black British citizen was present at these prayers, born in the Caribbean and representing the Pentecostal Church. I wondered whether he, too, was expected to say *Kyrie eleison* – and if so, on what basis? Had he acquired transmitted guilt along with his British and EC passport? Was he guilty simply by being a Christian? That seems a bit unfair, somehow. Was he exonerated on account of being black, and if so, is guilt colour-conscious? Might I as a child of Anglo-American revivalism half escape as being virtually mid-Atlantic?

My second illustration is taken from an article by Paul Oestreicher in the *Church Times* for 6th August 1995. Canon Oestreicher begins by recommending that we love and forgive our enemies. Naturally, I find no difficulty with that, particularly as I am not a victim and have no enemies to speak of. But then Canon Oestreicher extends the idea of forgiving enemies to the quite different idea of expressing contrition and offering forgiveness for corporate guilt. This idea has, he says, become a major theme among Christians, and he goes on to list some notable wrongs such as the Irish potato famine, Hiroshima, Dresden, the Treaty of Waitangi, British concentration camps in the Boer War and the Japanese invasions of China and Korea. Canon Oestreicher calls on us to choose between a corporate amnesia which buries the past, and taking up 'our' responsibility for the sins of our fathers and mothers. (I note that the Canon's political correctness now blames my mother as well as my father for the Irish potato famine. I also note that he uses the loose, broad categories I earlier complained of by referring to 'Japanese cruelty').

The trouble is that when we work out the implications of this rotating international ritual of contrition and forgiveness, we arrive at some astonishing scenarios. As we all start listing our corporate sins (with no historical cut-off point that I can see), we should presumably all repair to a venue designated by the United Nations. Once there, we begin what is in essence a secular version of the Last Judgment. In other words, just as the Christian categories of the individual and of man generically have been converted into the category of the nation, so the Last Judgment has been fast-forwarded out of eternity into secular time. Moreover, the divine Victim who is also the Judge is now a whole series of corporate victims, who apply not to the mercies of God, but to a judgment of history operated by historians.

Clearly, the universal day of collective atonements offers a bonanza to a whole class of appointed historians and conciliators, since one clearly has to make sure that all wrongs are properly revealed and their causes correctly identified. Nor will the selective list of standard crimes offered by Canon Oestreicher be remotely adequate to the demands of comprehensive justice. We must bring to book the Chinese dynasties, the Moghuls, the Incas, the Campbells, the political descendants of Vlad the Impaler, Tamerlane the Great, and Selim the Sot, the Albanians who massacred Greeks, the Greeks who expelled Muslim Cretans, the great-great-great grandchildren of Barbary Corsairs, and so on and on. This will be the Great Assize of all human infamy since the beginning of time.

Given the likelihood of disputes concerning the range of malpractice to be unveiled, the degree of responsibility incurred by various parties, and the relevance of extenuating circumstances such as provocation, a committee could be appointed, chaired by Professors Scruton and Hobsbawm, assisted by panels of approved victims nominated *inter alia* by Louis Farakhan, several Kurdish factions and the Armenian Liberation Front. At the end of it all, each of the High Forgiving Parties would bow solemnly to each other, receive and give absolution, and regard themselves as quits. And we could then start up all over again.

Before passing on I need to put down a marker concerning my own position. Contrition and forgiveness only make sense between persons or in relation to God, and they can only concern acts in which one is personally implicated through one's own deliberate fault or culpable negligence. Contrition and forgiveness may sometimes alter relations between persons even when only one party is so minded, and they must by definition do so when parties are mutually involved. But forgiveness between collectivities makes no sense and also makes no difference. The dynamic of redemption is not a moral technique to secure the better conduct of geo-politics. In the realm of international relations, nothing is likely to follow from gestures of forgiveness, even if they are noticed in the media, which is unlikely. To think otherwise is secular optimism glossed by Christianity.

Political and personal roles

What has been said so far can be summed up in a scenario off the beaten track of liberal exempla, which are generally drawn from a tiny group of modern ex-imperial democracies with longish histories as nations. What, however, might be the moral balance sheet between the governments and/or peoples of Sicily and Libya? How might one work out a tariff of contrition for Sicily to be offered to the Libyan dictatorship?

Sicily is an autonomous region of Italy, and from about 1911 to roughly 1941, Italy occupied Libya. The first question is: are the Sicilian people who were joined to Italy in recent times, and now have autonomy, responsible for the colonial ambitions of Italy, more particularly in its period of fascist government? The second question is: how do we trace the genealogy of Sicilian moral responsibility prior to Italian unification back through the Kingdom of the Two Sicilies and the Bourbons to the Normans and the Muslim Aghlabids based in North Africa? If it does not extend back in this way, what determines the cut-off point – geographical location in Sicily? Ethnicity? Religion? Regime? Type of regime? Or what?

A great deal of this muddle could have been avoided if the theology of Reinhold Niebuhr had been properly understood and permanently absorbed, particularly as set out in *Moral Man and Immoral Society* (1932). So, in a brief aside, I now need to rework Niebuhr in order to reinstate the difference between the moral dynamic of face-to-face relationships and relationships between collectivities. Let me now illustrate how a political role differs significantly from a personal role.

I begin with the order to a British submarine to sink the *General Belgrano* in the Falklands War of 1982. I happen to think this order morally unjustified and it may well be that the chain of decision can be traced to Mrs Thatcher and/or a small group of advisers. It could be that Mrs Thatcher herself came to view the order as unjustified, and said so, but that would be purely personal and of no great political significance.

The point is that wartime decisions are vested in small power élites, and there is an extended chain between major decisions and minute implementations. There is, therefore, a dispersal of moral responsibility. In the particular case of the *General Belgrano*, the decision was made in a complex political and military situation, where those concerned had to take rapid decisions by the minute.

155

It is, therefore, difficult to arrive at some moral accountancy and, moreover, any such accountancy would have to extend to the total situation.

Presumably, the prime objective of our theologians has to be moral justice to all parties, not just a specific judgment of one person's role. Justice would involve a moral assessment of all the actions on either side, reaching back from the immediate to the more distant past. Once that assessment is attempted, it becomes difficult to see how the chain of apology and contrition is to be set in motion. Who should apologize to whom for what? Perhaps General Galtieri should apologize to Mrs Thatcher, and she in turn to the parents of the drowned Argentinians. It is not clear how the cybernetic spiral of actions and reactions is to be unwound. Anyone who has heard the mutual recriminations of spouses can imagine how complex the issues must be once nations are involved.

All this is to say nothing of problems connected with the disavowal of Royal Navy servicemen, or contemporary political considerations which might inhibit or render counterproductive any attempt to unwind the moral and causal weave of that war. What is clear, however, is the non-involvement of the British as such in bringing about a state of war. It was not we as citizens who were the authors of the acts which gave rise to war.

Let me take another example. Similar problems would arise were one to propose an apology and contrition from the United Nations for failing to secure designated safe havens in Bosnia. It seems 'the' British preferred humanitarian responses to the overall situation, and so did the wrong thing for the right reason, just as the Americans in advocating military intervention did the right thing for rather doubtful reasons. Should, then, the British apologize for failing to kill more Serbs, and the Americans for killing a largish number of them?

As preliminary enquiries indicate, there is no way of apportioning blame within the complex resonating web of actions and reactions between the Secretary General of the United Nations, the various governments and the commanders in the field. We do suspect that direct responsibility lies with General Mladic, and if so that is where justice should be meted out.

The discussion above has already hinted that the possibility of apology depends on the nature of one's political role. Apologies by archbishops are as easy as they are meaningless, because they are not political players. Thus the Cardinal-Archbishop of Armagh may express regret for the deeds of the IRA which have nothing to do with him, but since the members of the IRA express no regret, it is not clear what his personal regrets can signify. A more interesting instance of the relation between political role and the range of regret one might feel able to express would be provided by John Hume MP. One needs to compare his generalized statements with the systematic political discourse of nationalist spokesmen of every variety. What they have to say is advanced under the rubric of peace, but the moment such phrases as 'all the people of this island', and 'a genuinely inclusive settlement' are used, it is implied that the wishes of the democratic majority in Northern Ireland are not decisive. That means violence, and thus peace has to be translated as war. Ambiguity and face-saving are of the essence and expressions of contrition would have immediately to be repudiated.

It goes without saying that all the players in this political dance must at some juncture be extremely economical with the truth. Consummate and principled hypocrisy is a *sine qua non* of political virtue in many situations. And that includes the refusal to break ranks and concede any more than is absolutely necessary. Those who break ranks are repudiated and those who concede more than is necessary offer propaganda opportunities to the opposing side. Each side has to pursue a policy of maximization in which survival depends on the maintenance of credit with one's own supporters, with the public and with the international community.

In short, corporate action works by semi-predictable game-plans whose rules are understood between the various conflicting parties, and rarely by moral gestures. The survival of corporate bodies turns on solidarities and minimal unities which bind members together *vis à vis* opponents. Each individual has, therefore, to be under a discipline that inhibits moral spontaneities, and this discipline constrains leaders as well as followers.

That applies in inter-party conflicts as well as international conflicts. In political debate in the House of Commons, for example, it is simply not an option for the leader of the Labour Party, however Christian he may be personally, to forgive the Conservative Party or to express contrition about the behaviour of his own party. Individual action is different from corporate action and that is why the Lord's Prayer does not apply across the floor of the House. Politicians are not there to forgive each other their trespasses or even to pay over-precise attention to the prohibition against false witness. Truth matters, yet too much endangers moral purposes.

Before looking at what Christianity might actually say, it is worth asking a question about the Bible, since Canon Oestreicher mainly justifies his position by reference to the Hebrew scriptures, although he also refers to that curious hybrid, Judaeo-Christianity. His argument is that the Bible treats cities and nations as corporate moral personalities and that God calls on them to repent as such. He adds that at the beginning of the parable of the sheep and the goats (Matthew 24:30), Christ refers to 'the nations' gathered before the Son of Man. But Oestreicher neglects to mention that the actual separation of the sheep from the goats is definitely not in terms of nationality.

Presumably, these Old Testament notions are open to rational critique among all non-fundamentalists. If, for example, God orders Achan's family to be stoned for the deeds of Achan, we dismiss the notion as primitive and unjust. The same applies to the divinely-inspired collective elimination of the Amalekites. We certainly do not promote such notions of corporate blame as the proper basis for contemporary law. Moreover, the story of God's mercy to Sodom and Gomorrah on account of the minority of just persons has very different implications. And even if peoples are called upon to repent before God, this seems rather different from being adjured on account of their bad behaviour to other nations. Unless my copies of the Bible are uniquely defective, I do not recollect prophecies commanding the

Israelites to apologize for ethnically cleansing the Amalekites, or for bringing indiscriminate plagues upon the Egyptians.

It is true that in his Gospel, St John does blame 'the people of the Jews' for various actions, but we can only assume that this is an example of the linguistic convention already mentioned, where a collective noun does duty for a group of individuals of a given ethnic group. Nevertheless, the history of anti-semitism shows just how dangerous such misleading locutions can be. Jews do not carry forward collective moral responsibility over time. Ezekiel chapter 18 is very clear on this point.

As for Christianity, it is one of those radical developments of Judaism which struggles to be free of this corporate, indeed biological membership, and stresses judgments based either in terms of personal responsibility, or on grounds of our incorporation 'in Adam' – that is, our status as human beings. Jesus is on the one hand genealogically rooted in Israel, but he is also the Son of Man, born not of the will of men but of the Spirit. He creates a universal fraternity based on the redemption of persons converted out of every kind of secular identification. That is precisely the point of Peter's confrontation with and conversion of Cornelius the Roman in the book of Acts, chapters 10 and 11.

The Christian understanding of forgiveness has to do with our separation from God in a radical self-love, and a self-interest which ignores the claims of others or exploits them for self-aggrandisement. This is sin and it inheres both in our corporate human constitution and in our individual brokenness. Though we are made in the image of God, that image is universally defaced, and we have ourselves through our own deliberate fault personally defaced it.

The consequences of defacement are to be viewed in the scarred visage of Christ, who by meeting enmity with love turned it to love's advantage. He absorbed our brokenness in the brokenness of his body, and so met the cost of reconciliation. Love's expense created the overflowing treasury of grace, from which we draw on a fiduciary basis – that is, solely by faith and trust. Nevertheless, we endeavour to respond to grace by ourselves leaning on grace in the power of the Spirit; to find ways of forgiving as we have been forgiven, and to ensure the spread of peace and justice.

This dynamic of redemption saves us, both communally and individually. As a redeemed community, we gather in family solidarity around the table, sharing the fruits of the common earth, bread and wine. These symbolically carry the freight of a shared redemption, since they represent both the broken body of sacrifice and our incorporation in reconciliation, wholeness and resurrected life. The same dynamic also saves us individually, by entering into our bodies and by washing us in the waters of baptism, ferrying us from darkness to light and from corruption to incorruption. Thereafter it becomes a duty, so far as may be, to institute the rule of the kingdom of heaven in the ordinary affairs of the city of man. At the heart of this city of man is now a recognition of disfigurement through the sign of the cross, and there are also elements of partial mutuality and self-giving, which faintly reflect the glory of the eternal city.

However – and this is the crux – the dynamic of redemption, coded in an enacted symbolism of breakage and restoration (the eucharist), which actually constitutes the Church, encounters a structural resistance inherent in collective action. The ravages of this resistance are reproduced simultaneously in the body of the Church and the body of society. They have to be countered by an everyday practical wisdom that is not itself written into the foundation charter of heaven's kingdom. This is because a foundation charter has to exhibit the fundamental images of sharing in the feast, including the outcast and uninvited, raising up the fallen, seeking the lost, restoring the sick, reconciling enemies and honouring the image of God in all his creatures and creation. These images indicate the standard and the goal, whereas it is left to practical wisdom to explore how far neighbourliness and caring can be built into the social fabric.

That exploration may involve some very varied and even paradoxical choices. Those choices emerge as the dynamism of redemption encounters the dynamism of our collective nature, represented by enmity, violence and the subordination of some people for the advantage of others. Politics can be the expression of an attempt to circumvent through the energies of practical reason these inbuilt resistances, fragmentations and subversions. But there can be no once-for-all redemption of the political, and that is as true today as it was 2000 years ago. The dynamism of redemption cannot be transferred to the political problems, except at the margin. The collective has its own social nature which allows it to build in some elements of morality and vision. That does not mean, however, that it constitutes a morally responsible (and therefore redeemable) corporate agency over time. If that were so, we would all be plunged for ever into irredeemable guilt.

The abuse of Christianity

In sum, the mistake of Christian utopianism is to conceive the *polis* as just such a corporate agent. That mistake represents an abuse of faith because it attempts simple transfers from the sphere of redemption to the sphere of politics. These transfers themselves damage redemption, turning it into a simplistic programme which mirrors secular categories and which shifts the Last Judgment from the realm of eschatology into an historical possibility. It hands justice over to historians and politicians. Christianity then becomes a mode of secular self-righteousness and denunciation, bypassing the careful assessment of different means of amelioration.

Should Christianity be fully secularized in the form of a once-for-all attempt to set up the kingdom on earth, either by exemplary violence or by exemplary non-violence, the problem is compounded. Neither has proved efficacious and the attempt collapses in confusions and ambiguities. It follows that it is impossible to read off political policies from the charter of the kingdom, though the potential presence of the kingdom and the judgment it represents remain the constant point of reference. The kingdom remains an iconography of compassion and warning.

The problem may be that Christianity has been partially released from the task of doubling for social authority. In carrying out that task, it reinforced repressive consciousness as well as decent orderliness and critical moral imagination. The contemporary release should allow Christianity a freedom to be itself, using the open texture and differentiated character of modern society. However, a partially footloose clerical intelligentsia has misconstrued this opportunity and reorganized Christian categories so as to transfer guilt and expiation to the sphere of the *polis*, leaving personal existence forlorn and untended.

People are urged to take responsibility for sins they could not have committed, and to treat those sins for which they are responsible as the externally imposed overflow of social structures. Thus, whereas in classical theology it is God who is the divine victim and bears the weight of sin in grace and love, in the new theology it is we who are the victims. But given the nature of society, we are fated to bear that with resentment and without expiation. That, indeed, is an abuse – not of religion, but of Christianity.

9

Towards an Executive Church

Should We Welcome the Turnbull Report?
Richard H. Roberts
In memoriam: David Gwyn Nicholls (1936-96)

The Church of England is in crisis. Falling membership, internal
dissension (not least over the ordination of women), the rapid
growth of so-called New Church congregations, the challenge of New
Age and neo-paganism, and the growing cultural dissonance
between a culture of individualistic hedonism and personal gain on
the one hand, and on the other, the ascetic and now societally
disfunctional ethos of Christianity – all of these are contributory
factors. The sudden and unexpected financial crisis caused by an
unfortunate property investment policy on the part of the Church
Commissioners created a situation in which a fundamental
reappraisal of the Church's function and purpose has at last become
possible.[1] A vacuum had to be filled, and the recent report of the
Archbishop's Commission on the organization of the Church of
England, *Working as One Body*, the so-called Turnbull Report,
proposes remedies of far-reaching significance which, when
implemented, may go far to fill this apparent void.

Drawing on the wider experience of society, the answer would
seem obvious: restructure the organization. While the defenders of
the report represent it as primarily concerned with efficiency and
accountability, my contention is that the proposed reforms are
natural corollaries of a larger pattern of social and cultural change,
the full consequences of which may be more far-reaching and
substantive than is at present realized.[2]

Working as One Body contains an innovative and brilliantly
conceived plan for the systematic restructuring of the Church of

England. Central to the report is a vision of the Church as an executive-led, highly unified organization, in many respects similar to a business corporation. There will in effect be a world president (the Archbishop of Canterbury), a company chairman (again the Archbishop of Canterbury), an executive board (the proposed national council of senior bishops and appointees) and a chief executive with considerable powers (the secretary general), and many leading positions will be occupied by archiepiscopal appointees. The plan involves the effective subordination of other important bodies to the executive. Most notably, General Synod will become an advisory and legislative body, representative of other stakeholders, which will (rather like the periodic meetings of shareholders in a public company) keep the executive in indirect touch with wider realities. The Church Commissioners will have a restricted financial function and be brought under executive remit.

Taken together, the Turnbull proposals are regarded by some as the most far-reaching changes to be enacted in the Church of England since the Reformation. Under the terms of the Turnbull Report, the national council will be the executive core of the Church. Theologically speaking, it might be difficult to resist the temptation to conclude that in reality it will also be the 'head' to which the body of the Church will be responsible. The very suggestion of this possibility has been denounced as 'blasphemy' by Bishop Turnbull.[3]

Again, as regards its relationship with contemporary England, it would be difficult to claim that *Working as One Body* is representative of more than a relatively narrow social constituency.[4] This should not be wholly surprising, given a commission consisting of senior clergy; business executives; a senior judge, civil servant and an academic; and selected General Synod representatives. The report therefore not only envisages a top-down model of the Church as regards the theological and managerial aspects of *episcope*, it also incorporates an implicit social hegemony. As such, all disclaimers of interest have (as in liberation theology) to be subject to ideological critique. Such a critique requires a deeper probing of the 'dialogue' between theology and organizational theory that infuses the report.

In this brief chapter, however, we subject *Working as One Body* to a preliminary contextual critique. Time will tell whether the normalization of the Church of England in terms of an ecclesiastical managerialism takes place, or whether this particular form of harmful religion is to be avoided.

The report says very little about the implications of structural changes for the overall 'culture' of the Church. While it denies that line-management is intended, informal field reports already indicate that the middle management of the Church (junior and suffragan bishops, archdeacons and rural deans) may well rapidly fall into line and assume the methods and demeanour associated with their newly defined roles.[5] Doubtless learning from practitioners in other commercial, business and service organizations, there may well be those who will build their careers on the basis of implementing the ecclesial equivalents of performance indicators – quality audit, pew customer charters, and so on – besides making sure that the Church's version of 'company loyalty' gently but surely stifles all dissenting voices.[6] The managerial culture offers both real power and 'empowerment' to its senior practitioners, and the seductive possibility of harnessing the motivation of others using religious and spiritual means.[7] Will anything be lost by these changes? Will the relative autonomy of the pastor survive in such an environment? Should we not welcome the remodelling of the Church according to the executive and managerial paradigm that has been imposed apparently with such success upon almost all other sectors of contemporary British society? Should the Church of England not be 'reformed' along with the National Health Service, the social services, the universities and all other areas of education? Are there any good reasons why the Church should not be thus 'normalized'?

In this chapter, we address questions in ways which some will without doubt find offensive. My primary purpose is to warn, both through drawing attention to parallels between *Working as One Body* and recent social and economic developments, and through outlining the likely consequences for the Church of England of an uncritical assimilation of these changes. Anyone familiar at first hand with what is involved in the contemporary 'reform' of the delivery of a range of human services, in an increasingly marketized environment will be aware that the separation of line management from means of detailed enforcement makes no sense at all. 'De-skilling', and thus the banalization (or 'MacDonaldization')[8] of the relation of 'provider' and 'customer' is the natural and even the inevitable partner of the contemporary integration of executive power.[9]

We proceed as follows: first, the rhetorical strategy of the content and public relations presentation of *Working as One Body* is subjected to critical examination. Second, the major proposals are outlined on the basis of a hermeneutics of suspicion, justified by the extraordinary and implausible claim that the only participants lacking any vested interest are the proponents of the scheme. Third, the theology of the report is interpreted in the light of its 'dialogue' with what the authors term 'organizational theory'.[10] Fourth, in conclusion, the implications of *Working as One Body* are drawn out in relation to the context of British (and world) society, in which 'managerialism' plays an ever-increasingly prominent role.

Rhetorical strategy

The report *Working as One Body* is a fascinating document, not least as regards its contextual presentation, structure and discourse. As an exercise in public relations, the mode of promulgation of the report embodies many features of contemporary managerial culture. Thus the provision of the text of the report itself (which is not an easy read for those unused to managerial newspeak), a flyer listing the Church's problems and the proposed solutions, and a cassette tape which presents the report in newscast form, to be played in parochial church councils, all come together as a package. The reader or hearer occupies a position similar to that of an employee, whose relatively passive role is to respond insofar as he or she facilitates the implementation of the policy. In reality, fundamental interrogation of such policy was neither desired nor envisaged.

It is important to remark upon the carefully wrought rhetorical structure of the document in which the shape of the text is reminiscent of that of a well-planned liturgy.[11] The Church's executive and managerial deficit is addressed in terms under which the managerial and organizational reform is implicitly sanctified through explicit references to the eucharistic context, to the 'theology of the gracious gift', and the invocation of the Holy Spirit.[12] Worthy of particular note, however, is the mixture of discourses. This could be illustrated at length, but the opening paragraph of the two Archbishops' foreword is representative. Those responsible for the report were invited:

> ...to recommend ways of strengthening the effectiveness of the Church's central policy making and resource direction machinery. They were encouraged not to shrink from radical ideas. Their report is forthright about the challenges which face the Church; much needs to be changed if the Church is to be effective as one body.[13]

The foreword continues in the same vein as the Archbishops write of creating a 'new mechanism', 'securing coherence', and moving 'purposefully to implement', in order to avoid 'prolonged uncertainty'. This discourse is of course that of the new managerial *classe dirigiste*, and this may have its place – even in a Church. There is an odd juxtaposition of this mechanical, functional language and the organic, theologically-derived image of the 'body'. The *topoi* of modern, Taylorian and human resources management co-exist with residual theological conceptions. Corresponding discursive sutures are evident at important points throughout *Working as One Body*; the text has the marks of skilful surgery directed towards the creation of a single-headed creature from diverse and contrasting raw parts. The Turnbull Report is thus representative of a distinctive, persuasive genre, and it incorporates in an all too obvious way fragments of discourse welded together by executive and managerial intent. In a strange way, *Working as One Body* is a classic example of conservative postmodern thinking.[14]

Hermeneutical suspicion

The societal setting of the particular assimilation of *topoi* drawn from theological and managerial in the text of *Working as One Body* is of paramount importance. We live in the era of the invasive metaphor. The discourse of management is but one form of rationality, driven forward by the stated need to control in order to secure accountability and cost-effectiveness (or so the argument goes). After all, as we are frequently told, managers must have the 'right to manage'. The managerial prerogative is not, however, the only, or the most important mode of rationality in human life – but such defensive claims are increasingly difficult to assert and sustain.[15] Nor, furthermore, should the uncriticized assertion of 'accountability' as the justification of enhanced control be regarded as value-free. On the contrary, an interest is being expressed and it is disingenuous for those responsible for the report to disclaim any such interest.

The implementation of the managerial revolution in contemporary Britain has proceeded with scant regard for the inherent integrity of the different spheres of human life that together make up aspects of a humane society. In the crudest terms, the much-quoted assertion of Margaret Thatcher, 'there is no such thing as society'[16] was a slogan indicative of a narrowing of perspective, a loss of the wisdom that respects the discreet integrity of human pursuits and a manifestation of an arrogance that assumes the right to reconfigure the lives of all those in society who are unable to buy their freedom in privatized personal services and congruent social isolation. In short, contemporary capitalism has been a progressively invasive power that in principle colonizes all dimensions of human life. Thus what begins as a set of challenging metaphors promoted at the margins in the original (and apparent) spirit of consultative experiment, becomes the means of an ongoing cultural transformation that redefines everything in its path.[17] So should religion remain unimproved – or unreformed according to the managerial imperative? Is the Church of England, apparently a most unlikely seat of transcendental freedom, now to conform to the 'reform' that cedes no limits to its subtle totalitarian power?

Given the fundamental changes in the relation of the public and private spheres on many levels since 1979, any individual in the context of organizations now faces the likelihood of the repeated reconfiguration of his or her personal identity. In such a setting, religion may offer one of the few areas of remaining societal space which possesses a continuing counter-cultural potential, despite (perhaps even because of) the archaic character of much mainline religious practice. On the other hand, the growing salience of religious or quasi-religious factors in contemporary social theory should be noted. We live in an era in which there is a complex and ambiguous 'return' or 'resurgence' of religion.[18]

Put more directly, when it is understood in the wider context, can the implementation of a managerial and executive revolution within the Church of England represent an embodiment of the righteous kingdom, not least in a society in which there are already poor safeguards for both individual and communitarian rights? Should societal conformity around the principles of managerialism – however much represented as secondary to mission goals – be extended into the Church, where radical Otherness may supposedly be encountered?[19] Where the Turnbull Report proposes a fundamentally uncritical assimilation of the Church's leadership and governance into the executive and managerial paradigm that now largely dominates British society, it promotes a foreclosure of the realm of ultimacy that relativizes all penultimates. The danger here is not that parishioners might be encouraged to worship mammon each Sunday, but that priests and ministers of the gospel are likely, given the implementation of the managerial paradigm, to respond to goals set for them, rather than responding to the high, difficult (and sometimes controversial) call to the responsible autonomy embraced by the authentic interpreter of religious tradition in any given socio-cultural context.

Thus, instead of exploring, learning and becoming critically responsive to the culture of a given ministry, they may simply adopt the identity and execute the role ascribed to them by managerial policy and thereby score many approval points on the relevant performance indicator ratings. In other words, once executive management becomes an end in itself, it is then easy and profitable for all institutional operatives simply to follow directives and relapse into rule-governed behaviour, rather than engage in demanding, critically-reflexive action.[20]

Theology and organization theory

It would be possible to expend considerable time and effort deciphering each paragraph of *Working as One Body*. In this section, we analyse briefly key themes which exemplify the uneasy synthesis between theological perspectives and those of management and organization theory. Reading on page 1 of the report, the recommendations of the Archbishop's Commission concern 'the life not of a business but of a Church in the Anglican tradition'. This tradition is characterized as one consisting in a combination of 'leadership by bishops with governance by synods representing bishops, clergy and laity', which 'avoids a large, centralized bureaucracy because it regards leadership as essentially the enablement of life and work in the dioceses, parishes and other spheres of Christian discipleship'.

Such a set of defining characteristics neatly subsumes leadership into an elite and defines the role of that elite in terms which elide the issue of power. The word 'enablement', along with the managerial favourite 'empowerment', is to be treated with healthy caution. This implicit treatment of power is further enlarged when the role of what we might call 'followership' is enlarged upon. Thus we are informed that the 'Anglican tradition calls for every member of the Church to share responsibility', because 'all must work together as one body'. The first part of paragraph 1.2 universalizes this obligation in relation to Christ's call to bear witness in what are regarded as 'compelling duties'. The second part of the paragraph transposes this universal sense of responsibility into what is termed a 'right relationship with those who discharge the responsibilities of leadership on behalf of the whole Church'. 'Proper accountability' and 'trust' are juxtaposed in the setting of what the Commission depicts as the 'theology of the gift': we must trust those whose gift is to lead. This, we are informed, is taught by our Anglican tradition.

The theological justification of comprehensive leadership and trusting followership is, however, at every point underpinned by 'organizational theory'. It would perhaps have been more transparent (but presentationally difficult) to have used the more obvious term 'management theory'.[21] It is at this juncture, in the understanding of power, that the theological and organization theoretical aspects of the Turnbull Report are deeply and not unproblematically intertwined. In succeeding paragraphs, the discourse of theology in 'polity' (1.4), God's relational and personal love for humanity (1.5), the trinitarian life of the Church (1.6), and the identification of the 'aims and tasks of the Church of England' with those of the 'one, holy, catholic and apostolic Church' (1.7) flows seamlessly.

In paragraph 1.8, the reader is suddenly informed that the Church 'must be a learning community'. Here once again, a key term of contemporary management theory, drawn from that of the 'learning organization',[22] is casually slipped in, to be followed immediately in 1.9 with an interesting suture of the two levels of discourse. Here we are informed that, 'the aims of the Church of England have already been given to it, it has continually to formulate and reformulate its specific *objectives* with a view to their being consistent with these fundamental aims and also being appropriate and relevant to the conditions of our land in our time'. Anyone who has attempted to separate the aims and objectives in the planning of any complex task will know how difficult it is to make a sharp distinction between the two. Here, however, much is at stake: who is to define these aims and objectives? Is this latter distinction an adequate basis for the connection between (as it were) the transcendental given and the immanent pragmatics? The power to define the terms of the discussion is transcendentally encoded in the argument: the reader's duty is that of receiver, and not questioner.

The integral logic of the remainder of 1.9 is clear: there is a stable 'given' which can be more or less efficiently transmitted in each generation. This is not theology as conceived in trinitarian terms, in which the Church exists in tension between act and fulfilment, straining towards an unpredefined future. On the contrary, here we are being confronted with an efficiency test which tacitly assumes a closure of, and thus control over, what is to be transmitted in witness as the 'given'. Thus – and this is characteristic of the discursive strategy of Working as One Body – a mass of loosely related theological material designed to resonate at the affective level of awareness is put into operation by key managerial and organizational terms which will actually orchestrate activity in the public world. In a sense, one might say (in reading back the managerial realism into the theological preamble) that the warehouses are full of the gospel; the problem is simply to shift the product in the most efficient and economically accountable way possible. Thus again another suture is apparent at the end of 1.9 where:

> To speak of the Church's 'direction' and 'effectiveness' (as do the terms of our enquiry) is to imply a grasp upon the mission which God has given to the Church; but at the same time it demands a critical and imaginative insight into current failures and future possibilities. What is asked of the Church at this particular moment is a combination of fidelity and expertise of various kinds in the formulation of its current objectives.[23]

Being translated, the last sentence means that a given aim (the gospel) requires new means to achieve its objectives (the delivery of that Gospel). We have here to pose the question: does this juxtaposition really reflect in an adequate way what Christianity and the Church are really about? The reality of the 'aim' underlying the text is that of an uncritically routinized charisma embodied in institutional practices which are legitimized by reference to 'tradition'.[24]

The task spelt out in 'objectives' is the pursuit of institutional and organizational efficiency, rather than active prophetic interpretation, or indeed the less spectacular but wholly central task of effective pastoral care, both of which require a degree of professional, relative autonomy and the exercise of much discernment. Moreover, if this analysis were to begin either with a theology of the laity (as in the 'people of God' strand of *Lumen Gentium*), or in an exploration of the ministerial remit at parish level, then the technique of presentation adopted in *Working as One Body* would appear even more implausible.

The Church and managerialism

The historian Edward Norman has argued that the episcopal elite in the Church of England has almost invariably tended to absorb and transmit the dominant ideology of its peer group.[25] This is now composed of the senior executives and managers who increasingly control all significant sectors of society. Thus a pillar-box Church is fed with ruling ideas from the top which percolate downwards in constant tension with the reality experienced at the base. Such cycles of assimilation have happened repeatedly since the emergence of political economy in the latter half of the eighteenth century.

What is now new about the present situation of the Church of England is that the ideology of managerialism being appropriated by its elite is infinitely more subtle and invasive than any of its clumsier predecessors. Indeed, the outstanding success of managerialism as an ideology is that it fights off all-comers with the charge that any resistance to the prerogatives and practices of managerial control is simply the expression of vested interests and an unwillingness to be efficient and accountable. The implementation of the latter almost invariably implies control.

While the basic rationale of the Turnbull Report expressed in terms of the need to gain efficiency may seem reasonable enough, in reality the 'managerial revolution' (to use James Burnham's resonant phrase)[26] involves sophisticated means of enforcement. It is part of the creeping sovietization of a managed, rather than an actively democratic Britain. Can we really believe that the advice that the Archbishop of Canterbury regularly receives from senior Christian executives and businessmen will allow that executive restructuring can be made fully effective without the consequential managerial practices affecting the whole organization? As Brian Mawhinney, Chairman of the Conservative Party in the Major administration, remarked on BBC Radio 4, reform is achieved through 'radical change followed by managerial enforcement'. The Church of England's present discourse as expressed in the Turnbull Report reflects all too clearly the tone of such means of change.

The scene is now set for the Church of England to step into line and conform with a national managerial revolution implemented with singular efficacy under John Major's premiership. Whereas Mrs Thatcher was confrontational (and the Church of England often responded in kind), Mr Major and his advisors knew well that managerial enforcement involves a highly differentiated process of de-skilling and the gradual stripping away of professional autonomy from middle-ranking employees. For the latter, the application of British Standard 5750 and ISO 9000 in quality audit normally involves the devising of intricate, self-imposed and internalized patterns of obediential behaviour. For the lower ranks, control is simply external and regulatory and the desired effects achieved through the behaviourist training schemes perfected in 'MacDonaldized' systems of product and service delivery. These are designed to achieve and enforce standards of uniformity in human behaviour previously only thought possible in mechanical production-line techniques.

Interestingly, managerial elites and management consultants worldwide have for some time been aware of the need to functionalize religion and spirituality in the workplace. This assimilation or 'synergesis' extends far beyond what many people are aware of. Now, when the barriers between modernity and religion are seemingly overcome, and spirituality is increasingly used as the basis for harnessing the most fundamental aspects of employees' motivation to institutional aims and objectives, mainline religion has to be ever more sensitive as to its societal role. Seen from the executive and managerial standpoint, the Church of England's sometimes seemingly unhelpful tendency to sustain a critical perspective upon a divided and imperfectly managed society (once more in evidence with the publication of *Staying in the City*)[27] would appear to require correction.

Rather than engage in fruitless confrontation, quiet advice whispered into the right episcopal ears, and a systematic restructuring of the Church in terms of an executive and subsequent managerial enforcement are far more effective. In more overt terms, the promulgation of a moral crusade directed at the regularization of behaviour by a return to traditional Christian values[28] falls within the range of desirable activities as understood from the executive and managerial standpoint, regardless of their intrinsic worth in a crisis-ridden society. Taken as whole, the proposals in the Turnbull Report, once properly supplemented with appropriate managerial control measures, will ensure not merely that social criticism should gradually cease, as it has in universities, but will also clear the way for the Church of England to become an efficient, product-led service organization, meeting the spiritual requirements of the residually Christian part of the English population with a regularized and marketable 'gospel'. In the words of Michael Novak, the 'empty shrine' of our particular form of capitalism will thereby be filled.[29]

Some forms of religious collective and self-expression remain for the moment among the few remaining spheres of human life which have resisted the invasive managerialism of contemporary Britain. Theology also remains a discourse – perhaps the only one remaining – which may still in the spirit of Dietrich Bonhoeffer erect barriers against the false ultimacy and infinite cunning of all totalitarian ideologies. In a society without a written constitution and sometimes lacking in a well-developed understanding of human rights, nothing less than our personal and collective identities are at stake. It will be a great pity if the Church of England silently falls into line and sacrifices the independence and responsible autonomy of its clergy and people on the altar of the false god of managerialism. This would be an unfortunate and self-imposed form of 'harmful religion'.

The price of spiritual freedom is perpetual vigilance, not least in the Church of England, which seems once again to seek accommodation with the spirit of the age. A superficial *via media* may be a course of action reflecting a tradition of Erastian conformity, rather than a creative reactivation of the challenge that true religion can make in the interests of the highest claims upon the human condition.

10

Jesus and the Thought Police

The Use and Abuse of 'Heresy'
Lawrence Osborn

'Tony Campolo is a theological liberal, a New Age pantheist, and a radical political socialist whose teachings are heretical at best and blasphemous at worst.'[1]

That is one fundamentalist's assessment of a well-known American evangelical. The aim of this chapter is to explore what is going on when such accusations are made and to offer various suggestions for the responsible use of the concept of heresy within Christian theology. First, by way of background, I shall briefly explore its traditional ecclesiastical usage.

What is heresy?

Heresy was given a rigorous definition by mediaeval canon law. It referred to the persistent and wilful denial of a defined doctrine of the Catholic faith by one who has been baptized and calls him or herself a Christian. This is a very narrow definition, perhaps too narrow to be useful in the long run. However, it does clearly distinguish heresy from various things that are not heresy, but are often confused with it.

For example, mere ignorance is not heresy. A person who denied some aspect of the faith because of inadequate instruction was not held culpable. Heresy had to be persistent and wilful: a viewpoint maintained in the face of formal instruction and, where appropriate, theological debate. Nor is one who has entirely abandoned the Christian faith a heretic. Such a person is properly designated an apostate. Apostasy has in its favour a certain clarity. The apostate has abandoned that particular language game altogether. By contrast, the heretic wants to continue playing the game but with a different set of rules (like the soccer player who wants to be able to pick up the ball and run with it – and still call the game soccer, rather than rugby).

Again, the term heresy does not apply to heterodox statements made by non-Christians. A heretic must have received Christian baptism and must publicly claim to be part of the body of Christ. Thus the Christological assertions of a member of the Liberal Catholic Church should not be regarded as heretical, since he or she belongs to a theosophical organization with no recognized organic connection to Catholic Christianity. Of course, such restrictions in the meaning of the term have not stopped Christians from misusing it against their opponents. Thus we come across plentiful medieval references to 'Jews and other heretics', or 'Mohammedans and other heretics'.

This narrow definition of heresy also distinguishes between heresy and schism. Such a distinction has been made since at least the fourth century. Thus, for example, Augustine defined heretics as those who 'in holding false opinions regarding God, do injury to the faith itself,' as distinguished from schismatics, who 'in wicked separations break off from brotherly charity, although they may believe just what we believe'.

Similarly, Basil of Caesarea regarded heretics as 'men who were altogether broken off and alienated in matters relating to the actual faith,' and schismatics as 'men who had separated for some ecclesiastical reasons and questions capable of mutual solution.'[2] However, this distinction between mere ecclesiastical dispute and heresy has been singularly difficult to maintain in practice. Take, for example, the Great Schism between Roman Catholicism and Orthodoxy. Similarly, the cases of Montanism and Donatism reveal the inevitable interweaving of ecclesiastical and doctrinal questions.

It is worth noting that the earliest Church did not make such a distinction. On the rare occasions when the term heresy appears in the New Testament, it seems virtually synonymous with factionalism (see Romans 16:17; 1 Corinthians 11:18f; Galatians 5:20). The problem existed before the emergence of clearly articulated Christian doctrines and can pertain to aspects of the Church's life where no doctrine has yet been articulated.

This suggests that the legal definition of heresy addresses the symptoms rather than the root cause. The close connection between heresy and factionalism points to the denial or destruction of Christian unity as the underlying problem. Thus, at root, heresy is the wilful breaking of the body of Christ. It is the subversion of the life of the Christian community. It is important to clarify what this means. Otherwise the door would be open for an ecclesiastical establishment to define any questioning of its power structures as heresy. Questioning the particular forms of the Church's life is not necessarily heretical. Heresy arises only when the very life of the Church is called into question.

The Church is the community of the promise of the Kingdom of God. It exists to articulate that promise and as the anticipation of the promise's fulfilment. Therefore the reality of the Church lies in mission. In the words of Robert Jenson: 'the Church is sent to get a specific word said in the world'.[3] Thus, heresy is an assault upon the Church's role as bearer of the divine promise.

This implies that theological innovation is not, in itself, heretical. Mere deviation from a doctrinal consensus or the use of neologisms should not be construed as heresy. On the contrary, Christian orthodoxy is dynamic. This is so because Christianity involves the proclamation of the good news of Jesus Christ to men and women of every culture and age. Furthermore, that proclamation takes the specific form of translation. It is an inherent part of Christianity that every language and culture is a potential bearer of the promise of the kingdom. There is no such thing as a unique distinctively Christian culture. Christian orthodoxy has to change in order to remain true to itself.

It is, of course, in that process of change that heresy is most likely to arise. The challenge of translating the gospel into forms appropriate to a new culture forces us to experiment, and sometimes we get it wrong. In attempting to make the gospel relevant to its hearers, we go beyond the bounds of legitimate creativity and distort the substance of the Christian proclamation.

One recurring way in which this has happened is by losing the tension between the gospel and the culture. Every culture can be a bearer of the gospel, but equally every culture is challenged differently by the gospel. When that tension is lost, Christianity degenerates into religious nationalism. The history of Christianity is littered with examples from medieval Christendom, through the imperialism of many nineteenth-century missionaries, to the German Christianity, Serbian Orthodoxy and Croatian Catholicism of our own century.

On the other hand, precisely because orthodoxy is dynamic, we dare not take refuge in a static body of clearly defined doctrine. To do so is to absolutize a particular form of the gospel. It is to set up a particular human interpretation of the gospel as final. There is such a thing as a heretical traditionalism that, while maintaining the form of the gospel, denies its substance (perhaps by making it incomprehensible to a new generation or a different culture).

It follows that what constitutes heresy cannot be determined by a simple test against a static rule of faith. This is not only because heresy and orthodoxy are both dynamic, but because a particular heresy need not have been given rational expression to be at work. Belief and practice are inseparable. Thus, for example, it is not just theological justifications of apartheid or slavery that fully deserve the label 'heresy'. Even before those justifications were articulated, the men and women practising slavery while professing Christianity were already betraying the Christian gospel by their practice.

The charge of heresy as religious abuse

And so to a consideration of the misuse of heresy charges. To clarify the function of heresy charges at least in some ecclesiastical contexts, I shall outline several transparently malicious examples. Precisely because they are so plainly malicious, they show very clearly how such charges function as religious abuse.

My first source is an American attorney, Constance Cumbey, who has earned a certain notoriety as a particularly outspoken critic of the New Age movement. In the course of her assault upon the New Age, she takes issue with several evangelical Christians whose political agenda differs from her own. Among those attacked for being soft on the New Age (if not covert allies of the New Age) are Inter-Varsity Fellowship, World Vision and Ron Sider (author of the influential book, *Rich Christians in an Age of Hunger*).

She also attacks Loren Wilkinson and the fellows of the Calvin Center for Christian Scholarship 1977-78 for their scholarly examination of the environmental crisis from an evangelical perspective. A quite specific heresy charge is laid at their door in that while professing to be evangelical Christians they are in fact advocating 'Hindu occultism'.[4] In fact, the specific charge is based on the deliberate misrepresentation of a passage in their report where they express sympathy for an aspect of Eastern Orthodox theology.[5] Cumbey does not explain her own environmental agenda, but, from comments she makes in passing, it is plain that she sees the environmental crisis merely as another piece of evidence that the return of Christ is imminent. Thus, for her, the appropriate response is not environmentalism, but evangelism. The most charitable interpretation of her outlook is that she regards Christian environmentalism as a culpable diversion from the task of proclaiming the gospel.

Cumbey has also made outspoken attacks on other conservative evangelical cult watchers. She is particularly critical of the Spiritual Counterfeits Project and the Christian Research Institute. In her view, both organizations are guilty of misleading Christians as to the extent of the threat posed by the New Age movement. She has also accused them of promoting New Age ideas. As in the case of Loren Wilkinson and his colleagues, her accusation can be shown to be a tissue of deliberate defamation woven from a mixture of innuendo, faulty logic and falsehoods.[6] It so happens that both groups have been very critical of Cumbey's approach to new religions and have questioned her competence as a researcher.

In both cases, an implicit accusation of heresy has been used as a weapon to undermine the influence of others. In the case of the Calvin Fellows, Cumbey is seeking to undermine a political/ environmental agenda that differs from her own because it is informed by a different eschatology. In the case of the anti-cult groups, she is simply attacking senior competitors in her own field.

Other contemporary heresy charges within the American evangelical community display a similar combination of purposes: an attempt to marginalize an influential opponent and defend a very specific doctrinal emphasis (usually pre-millennialism or biblical inerrancy).

Take the recent attack on Tony Campolo. He is perceived as politically left of centre in that he is committed to the pursuit of social justice as an integral part of the proclamation of the gospel. As with Constance Cumbey's various accusations, underlying the different political outlook there may be a different eschatological perspective (post-millennialism is a more satisfactory eschatology for social activists than pre-millennialism). Again the goal is to undermine an opponent by whatever means. In Campolo's case, the tactics of his opponents have included issuing false press releases claiming to come from gay rights groups endorsing Campolo's views. They have perhaps learned to avoid direct confrontation with him, since an earlier heresy charge against him had to be withdrawn after a tribunal of prominent evangelical theologians concluded that, while some of his statements lacked clarity, he was not heretical.

Similar attacks have been made upon prominent evangelicals who are perceived as having absorbed ideas from psychoanalysis, particularly in its Jungian form. This lay at the heart of fundamentalist attacks on James Dobson and the evangelical broadcaster Karen Burton Mains. Mains also stands accused of being associated with Renovaré (a renewal movement founded by

Richard Foster), and of receiving spiritual direction from a Roman Catholic. Her detractors are quite explicit about the fact that they are motivated by a desire to defend the doctrine of biblical inerrancy.

Inerrancy also lies at the heart of the accusations against Howard van Til. Van Til is a physics professor at Calvin College in Michigan and a prominent member of the American Scientific Affiliation (the North American counterpart of Christians in Science). He has made no secret of the fact that he is a theistic evolutionist and he has been publicly critical of the scientific status of so-called creation science. The outcome of his stance was that he became the defendant in a heresy trial within the conservative reformed Church of which he is a member. Like the earlier Campolo case, the judicial setting enabled van Til to defend himself against the accusations, and he was subsequently acquitted.

What does an accusation of heresy do? It clearly alters the nature of a (theological) disagreement. A disagreement is a direct personal confrontation between two people. The effect of the heresy charge is to objectify the confrontation and to make it less direct. It is no longer the case that A disagrees with B. Rather, A affirms his adherence to C (where C is the constitutive authority of the community – scripture, creeds, confessions, articles, etc.) and notes with dismay B's lack of adherence at certain points.

A heresy charge marginalizes the person accused by presenting that person as in conflict with the very basis of the community to which they belong. It undermines their voice and their standing within the community. It implies that they have wittingly or unwittingly aligned themselves with falsehood, evil and the Devil. I commented earlier that heresy is properly applicable only to members of one's own religious community. To a Muslim, I am an infidel rather than a heretic (and vice versa). However, one can see how useful the charge of heresy is in dissuading members of one's own community from listening to voices of which one does not approve.

Conversely, a heresy charge has the effect of strengthening the position of the person who makes the charge. This is because, in making the accusation, he or she is not merely saying 'I disagree with that person', but rather, 'I am in wholehearted agreement with the authority that underpins our community'. In consigning the other person to the outer darkness, I am aligning myself with the light; I am publicly affirming my commitment to truth, good and God.

Furthermore, in those communities which have a high regard for their constitutive authority, heresy accusations are a winning strategy. Even if the accusation is subsequently shown to be wrong, it leaves the accuser in a stronger position. After all, if I have mistakenly accused you of heresy, it merely shows that I have perhaps been a little over-zealous in my defence of the truth. Its function in publicly aligning me with the authority at the heart of the community is not affected by the mere fact that I got it wrong this time. As for the accused, their position is inevitably weakened by the fact that people could question their commitment to that authority. 'There's no smoke without fire...'

It follows from what I have been saying that certain religious environments are more prone to heresy charges than others. Rubem Alves has done a masterly job in describing and analysing one such environment in his book, *Protestantism and Repression*.[7] In it, he describes the impact of an extreme conservative evangelicalism, which he denotes 'Right Doctrine Protestantism', upon the Reformed Church in Brazil.

Entry into this community is by way of an intense religious experience – a conversion experience – which undermines one's previous world view. However, that experience is no more than an entry point. Nothing as subjective as religious experience is permitted to influence the world view of the community. On the contrary, the new convert is cast in the role of passive recipient to be catechized. Conversion is not an adequate basis for membership of such a community. Only when the convert can make a public confession of adherence to a static body of clearly articulated doctrines is he or she regarded as a member of the body of Christ. In such an environment, questions, doubts and even alternative modes of expressing orthodoxy are perceived as attacks on the world view that forms the basis of the community. Even a small deviation from the doctrinal consensus becomes a threat to the life of the community.

Ironically, in their zeal to maintain orthodoxy, such communities have effectively become gnostic in their outlook. They may maintain that salvation is by faith in Christ, but that is severely qualified by their insistence that adequate knowledge is essential to full participation in the life of the body of Christ. And because of the shift of emphasis from faith to knowledge, such communities also tend to be internally elitist and externally exclusive.

Alves describes an extreme case, but his analysis applies to many less extreme Christian groups in the United Kingdom and North America. It is the ideal environment for the generation of heresy charges – a community constituted by a clearly articulated authoritative body of knowledge.

However, heresy charges do not merely spring from such an environment. They also reinforce it. They create a climate in which divergence from the community consensus is more difficult. Criticism of those in authority also becomes more difficult in such a climate. The community and its leaders perceive such divergence and criticism as an attack on God's work.

For example, an episcopalian theologian, William DeArteaga, recently gave a talk on heresy to a gathering of Christian leaders at the then Toronto Airport Vineyard. In the talk, he redefined heresy as the pharisaical criticism of revival movements such as the Toronto Blessing, and cited the Christian Research Institute as an example, because of its uneasiness about certain aspects of Toronto. In similar vein are some 'prophecies' circulating within Toronto Blessing circles in direct response to criticism by other Christians. For example: 'There will be those who call themselves by my name and who try to stand against my work. They will most surely fall and will be pushed into the sand. My work will be accomplished.'

The deconstruction of 'heresy'

In view of the widespread abuse of heresy charges, it is tempting to conclude that an accusation of heresy is always a covert assertion of power over the other. That of course was precisely Bauer's thesis in his classical account of orthodoxy and heresy in the early Church. It is an accusation that re-emerges in, for example, Elaine Pagels' work on Gnosticism. As befits one who has adopted a liberationist perspective, Rubem Alves also subscribes to this thesis. Thus:

> The orthodox are those who had the political power to impose their definitions. Thus orthodoxy always embodies the ideas of the stronger. By the same token heresy points to the ideas of those who were weaker, who did not have the political power to impose their definitions on the ecclesiastical community. In the last analysis, the definition of truth is a question of power.[8]

This is a characteristically modern way of looking at truth and authority. It reaches its full flowering in Nietzsche's insistence that all truth claims are covert power claims, and postmodernism's insinuation that all metanarratives are inherently oppressive. However, it is already apparent in the Enlightenment's attack upon authority and tradition in the name of human autonomy and reason. One outcome of this has been that heresy is seen in an entirely new light. Far from being a term of opprobrium, heresy can now be a term of approval. The heretic is cast in the role of hero: a brave individual who boldly maintains his or her own opinions despite all the efforts of a repressive establishment. Every dissenter is now a potential Luther: 'Here stand I. I can do no other. God help me. Amen.'

In those Churches that have been most successful in adapting to post-Enlightenment culture, this has resulted in an effective reversal of the function of heresy charges. Concerns about orthodoxy may be seen as an attempt to stifle creativity. If I wonder aloud about another theologian's orthodoxy, I am liable to be seen as siding with the forces of reaction in an attempt to stifle legitimate theological enquiry.

In such an environment, theologians and ministers are understandably reluctant to comment critically on the orthodoxy of others. They know that they are liable to be marginalized. At best, they may be dismissed as part of the Church's lunatic fringe. They may find themselves discriminated against by the ecclesiastical establishment. Or their motives may be called into question. Take, for example, the case of Gareth Bennett. Some years ago, he was invited to contribute the traditional anonymous preface to *Crockford's Clerical Directory*. His offering was highly critical of the liberal establishment in the Church of England. The subsequent hue and cry which led to Bennett's suicide revealed the 'liberal' establishment to be every bit as abusive in its pursuit of outspoken orthodoxy as any rabid fundamentalist in pursuit of heresy.

Reclaiming 'heresy'

I will admit to having a certain sympathy for the deconstructive approach to heresy. Many heresy accusations can be shown to be assertions of power. In particular, I am inclined to suspect that heresy charges are being used abusively when they are used by those in positions of ecclesiastical power to control or limit the influence of named individuals.

Anyone who believes that the concept of heresy is of value in today's Church effectively faces a two-pronged attack. On the one hand, we have the liberal establishment of the major denominations questioning the integrity of those who make heresy charges. On the other, we have conservative Christians apparently displaying precisely what the liberal establishment fears.

Nevertheless, the history of Christianity is littered with examples of theological creativity, missionary zeal, or ecclesiastical self-interest that have gone as far as to subvert the very substance of the Christian gospel. By what other name should we call the efforts of German Christians to baptize Nazism, or the theological justifications of apartheid by white South African Christians? In view of such examples, I am convinced that there is still a need for the concept of heresy within Christian theology. Clearly, there is also a need for guidelines to promote the responsible use of the concept. How should I respond if I am concerned that a particular teaching or practice within my church may be heretical?

As the beginning of an answer, we may usefully recall a meeting that took place in May 1934 in the little German town of Barmen. Delegates of the German Evangelical Church (an umbrella organization that incorporated the Lutheran, Reformed and United Churches) gathered to discuss their growing concern over the teaching and behaviour of the Church leadership. Specifically, they were disturbed by the efforts of those leaders to align the Protestant Churches with the principles and programmes of Nazism. At the end of the meeting, they unanimously approved a six-point declaration, reaffirming the theological basis of the German Evangelical Church and naming as false doctrine certain key teachings of the Church leadership.

Whatever its limitations as a response to the political situation of the day, I believe Barmen can function as a model of an appropriate Christian response to heresy. To begin with, it is a corporate response to the teaching and action of an influential group within the German Evangelical Church. The people involved on both sides were the official representatives of their Churches.

Heresy is essentially a corporate matter. We are often told that the root meaning of heresy is choice. This is true, but it is not choice in the sense of private opinion; it is choice in the sense of a school of thought (or a corporate practice) which strikes at the heart of the Christian gospel. The private opinions of individual Christians are not an appropriate target for heresy charges. This is reflected in the traditional principle, *salvo jure diversa sentira* – the Catholic Church can accommodate a diversity of private opinions. Tolerance of private doctrinal idiosyncrasy is one mark of catholicity. Conversely, intolerance of private opinions that diverge from the public consensus is symptomatic of sectarianism.

Similarly, the appropriate response to heresy will be corporate. It is not the task of the individual theologian or minister to engage in heresy hunting. Heresy charges are a matter for the Church as whole, and not for individuals. Karl Barth, who was responsible for drafting the Barmen Declaration, is quite unequivocal on this point: 'It cannot be the business of dogmatics to establish and proscribe a new heresy as such, to stigmatize individual personalities and movements in the Church as heretical, i.e. as standing outside the Church.'[9] While he insisted that it is part of the legitimate task of theology to oppose theological error, the denunciation of such errors as heretical must be left to the wider Church.

Secondly, the Barmen Declaration was the result of a process of prayerful theological discussion. The influence of the German Christians had been growing for several years – a period during which the uneasiness of the Barmen delegates had been growing. In that time, they had subjected their opponents' views to critical examination and gave good theological reasons for their uneasiness. With the benefit of hindsight, we may be inclined to dismiss Barmen as 'too little, too late'. However, I believe the principle is sound. Indeed, I think it can be discerned at work in Paul's correspondence with the Corinthian church.

Paul perceives error within the church and responds by engaging in public debate – explaining the nature of their errors and responding with his understanding of Christian truth. This contrasts sharply with his response to immorality: 'It is actually reported that there is sexual immorality among you, and of a kind that does not occur even among pagans: A man has his father's wife. And you are proud! Shouldn't you rather have been filled with grief and have put out of your fellowship the man who did this?' (1 Corinthians 5:1-2).

If we suspect heresy, we should not respond by excommunicating the suspect. Rather, we should engage in theological discussion, seeking to understand the other side and discern where the truth lies. This is a reminder that heresy has often been the catalyst for a more careful articulation of theological truth. Indeed, on occasion, a thought-provoking heresy may be more helpful to the Church than a comforting restatement of the doctrinal consensus.

If reconciliation is clearly impossible, the Barmen Declaration again acts as a model for the way to proceed. It is not merely a negative denunciation of doctrines perceived to be false. Nor does it attack individual Christians who might subscribe to those doctrines. Rather, it points its readers back to fundamental Christian truths and draws implications from those truths for a response to Nazi ideology. Take, for example, the Fourth Article:

> 'You know that the rulers of the Gentiles lord it over them, and their great men exercise authority over them. It shall not be so among you; but whoever would be great among you must be your servant.' (Matthew 20:25-26.)
>
> The various offices in the Church do not establish authority of some over others; rather, they exercise the ministry entrusted and commanded to the whole congregation. We reject the false doctrine that the Church, apart from this ministry, could and were permitted to give to itself, or is allowed to have given to it, special leaders, vested with powers to rule.[10]

It is incumbent upon those bringing heresy charges not merely to denounce the errors they perceive in others, but to engage in the more exacting task of stating fundamental Christian truth for the situation in which they find themselves. Nor can this merely be a restatement of an earlier creed or confession, for the reasons given earlier.

To summarize: if we wish to act responsibly in bringing heresy charges against a particular doctrine or practice, we must work with others, representative of the wider Church; we must engage in a process of prayerful theological debate with our opponents. At the end, if our differences have not been resolved by the process of dialogue, we should continue by way of a constructive statement of what we perceive to be fundamental Christian truth, and the ways in which the opposing position contradicts that truth.

Notes

Notes to Introduction

1. FitzSimmons Allison, C., *The Cruelty of Heresy* (SPCK, London, 1995).

2. For the viewpoint of an investigative journalist, see Howard, R., *The Rise and the Fall of the Nine O'Clock Service: A Cult Within the Church?* (Cassell, London, 1996).

3. The most critical and academic look at Wimber is to be found in Percy, M., *Words, Wonders and Power: Understanding Contemporary Christian Fundamentalism and Revivalism* (SPCK, London, 1996).

4. At the time of going to press, the Church of England is considering a formal enquiry into the Nine O'Clock Service.

5. See Howard, *op. cit.*

6. Peter Berger has turned this argument on its head and has suggested that Christian religion is itself heresy in the face of secular modernity. See Berger, P., *The Heretical Imperative: Contemporary Possibilities of Religious Affirmation* (Collins, London, 1980).

7. London, BCC publications, 1990.

8. Los Angeles, Jeremy, P. Tarcher Inc., 1991.

9. Our collected papers and conversations were later published. See Smail, T., Walker, A., Wright, N., *Charismatic Renewal: The Search for a Theology* (SPCK, London, second edition 1995).

10. Walker, A., *Restoring the Kingdom: The Radical Christianity of the House Church Movement* (Hodder & Stoughton, London, second edition 1988), p. 346.

11. Rev. Bernard Green, the former General Secretary of the Baptist Union, for example. See Walker, A., *op. cit.*, p. 272.

12. In unpublished remarks to the author in his office in Clarendon Villas, Hove, June 1989.

13. Although some of the New Churches, New Frontiers, for example, tend to have large congregations, their overall numbers are still tiny in comparison with Anglicanism or Methodism.

14. There is, however, a legitimate tradition in Christianity of voluntarily accepting collective guilt. The Old Testament story of Nehemiah is one of a man who took responsibility for the nation upon his own shoulders.

15. Foucault, M., *Madness and Civilization: a History of Insanity in the Age of Reason* (trans. from the French by Howard, R., Routledge, London, 1990).

Notes to Chapter 1
Religious Abuse

1. HMSO, May 1989.

2. Knox and Vidler, *The Gospel of God and the Authority of the Church*, p. 106.

3. Gratieux, A., *Khomiakhov et le Mouvement Slavophile,* Tome II: *Les Doctrines*, p. 111.

4. *New Religious Movements*, General Synod Paper, (GS Misc 317, Church House, Great Smith Street, 1989).

5. *Mission, Dialogue and Inter-Religious Encounter*, pp. 12f.

Notes to Chapter 2
Shepherding: Care or Control?

1. Walker, A., *Restoring the Kingdom* (Hodder & Stoughton, 1985).

2. Tarleton, G., *Birth of a Christian Anarchist* (Pendragon Press, 1993), pp. 68-72.

3. Avis, P., *Authority, Leadership and Conflict in the Church* (Mowbray, 1972), pp. 67-70.

4. Nee, W., *The Normal Christian Church Life* (International Students Press, Washington, 1962).

5. Nee, W., *Spiritual Authority* (Christian Fellowship Publishers, 1972), p. 71.

6. Ortiz, J.C., *Disciple* (Lakeland, 1975), pp. 100-117. Interestingly, Ortiz has now completely abandoned the doctrine of discipleship.

7. Prince, D., *Discipleship, Shepherding, Commitment* (Derek Prince Publications, 1976) pp. 32-35.

8. All names in this section have been changed.

9. Kepel, G., *The Revenge of God* (Polity Press, 1994), pp. 1-12.

10. Peck, S., *The Different Drum* (Arrow Books, 1990), pp. 187-200.

11. Tomlinson, D., *The Post-Evangelical* (Triangle, 1995) pp. 47-59.

Notes to Chapter 3
Giving the Devil More Than His Due

1. Richards, J., 'The Barnsley Case: Confusion of Thought', *Church Times*, 18th April, 1975.

2. Wright, N., *The Fair Face of Evil* (Marshall Pickering, London, 1989) p. 124.

3. Hunt, S., 'Deliverance: The Evolution of a Doctrine', *Themelios*, 21:1, 1995, pp. 10-13.

4. Walker, A., 'The Devil You Think You Know: Demonology and the Charismatic Movement', in Smail, T., Wright, N. and Walker, A., *Charismatic Renewal: The Search for a Theology* (SPCK, London, 1993) pp. 86-105.

5. 'Deliverance from Evil', in *Redemption* (Assemblies of God, February 1990) pp. 13-17. Also in the same edition, 'The Battle is On', which critically looks at the ministry of Bill Subritsky, pp. 5-7. For a conservative evangelical critique, see Masters, P., *The Healing*

Epidemic (Wakeman, London, 1989) pp. 109-11; Morrison, A., *The Serpent and the Cross: Religion and Corruption in an Evil Age* (K&M Books, Birmingham, 1994) pp. 504-14.

6. Wimber, J. with Springer, K., *Power Healing* (Hodder & Stoughton, London, 1986).

7. Berger, P., *The Social Reality of Religion* (Faber & Faber, London, 1967).

8. Perry, M., *Deliverance: Psychic Disturbances and Occultist Involvement* (SPCK, London, 1987, new edition, 1996).

9. Pattison, S., *Alive and Kicking: Towards a Practical Theology of Healing* (SCM, London, 1989) pp. 163-65.

10. Powell, G. and S., *Christian Set Yourself Free* (New Wine Press, Chichester, 1983).

11. See Wright, N., *op. cit.*, especially chapter 1.

12. Kapferer, B., *A Celebration of Demons: Exorcism and Aesthetics in Sri Lanka* (Indiana University Press, Bloomington, 1983).

13. Oesterrich, T.K., *Possession, Demonical and Other Among Primitive Races of Antiquity* (London, 1930).

Notes to Chapter 4
Healing Ministries and their Potential for Harm

1. Cassidy, Sheila, *Sharing the Darkness* (Darton, Longman & Todd, London, 1989), p. 64.

2. Pooley, Jane, and Wood, David, in their article 'Rituals: the Power to Damage and the Power to Heal', quoted in *Treating Survivors of Satanist Abuse*, edited by Valerie Sinason (Routledge, London, 1994), p. 27.

3. Maddocks, Morris, *The Christian Healing Ministry* (SPCK, London, 1985), p. 138.

4. *Ibid.*, p. 9.

Notes to Chapter 5
The Other Side of Joy

1. For an excellent discussion of these issues, see Schumaker, John F., *Religion and Mental Health* (Oxford University Press, New York, 1992).

2. For a more detailed examination of Protestant vocation, religious personality and 'religiously-grounded selfhood,' see Rubin, Julius H., *Religious Melancholy and Protestant Experience in America* (Oxford University Press, New York), pp. 12-21.

3. See Clines, Francis X., 'Sect's Tenet: Thou Shalt Not Traffic in Demon Gossip', *The New York Times*, 2nd March 1995; Hollyday, Joyce, 'The Stuff of Life: A Visit to the Bruderhof', *Sojourners*, Vol. 13, No. 5, May 1984; Nash, Connie, 'Bruderhof Women: A Testimony of Love', *Other Side*, Vol. 22, No. 5, August 1986; Rice, Judith, 'Hutterians', *History Today*, Vol. 44, No. 7, 1994.

4. The Bruderhof have long characterized themselves as joyful. See Zablocki, Benjamin, *The Joyful Community* (Penguin Books, Baltimore, 1971); Whitworth, John McKelvie, *God's Blueprints: A Sociological Study of Three Utopian Communities* (Routledge & Kegan Paul, Boston, 1975); Oved, Iaacov, *Witness of the Brothers: A History of the Bruderhof* (Transaction, New Brunswick, 1996).

5. Mow, Merrill, *Torches Rekindled: The Bruderhof's Struggle for Renewal* (Plough Publishing House, New York, 1989), pp. 124-25.

6. Parsons, Arthur S., 'The Secular Contribution to Religious Innovation: A Case Study of the Unification Church' (*Sociological Analysis*, Vol. 50, No. 3, p. 210).

7. *Children in Community* (Plough Publishing House, New York, 1963), p. 99.

8. See the autobiography of a former member, Pleil, Nadine Moonje, *Free From Bondage* (Carrier Pigeon Press, San Francisco, 1994), pp. 219ff.

9. Accounts of childhood clearances can be found in the KIT Newsletter, PO Box 460141, San Francisco, CA, 94146, USA, or through the Internet site: http://www.matisse.net/~peregrin/

10. Stoeffler, F. Ernest, *German Pietism During the Eighteenth Century* (Temple University Press, Philadelphia, 1973), pp. 12-16.

11. Bonhoeffer, Dietrich, *The Cost of Discipleship* (MacMillan, New York, 1963), p. 100.

12. Arnold, Heini, *Freedom From Sinful Thoughts: Christ Alone Breaks the Curse* (Plough Publishing House, New York, 1973), p. 1.

13. Mow, *op. cit.*, p. 127.

14. Arnold, *op. cit.*, p. viii.

15. Ramon Sender, see http://w.w.w.matisse.net/~peregrin/

16. The story of Faith is quoted from an unpublished testimony and used here with permission of the author.

17. See Jacobs, Janet Liebman, *Divine Disenchantment: Deconverting from New Religions* (Indiana University Press, Bloomington, 1989).

Notes to Chapter 6
Theology and Political Correctness

1. By taking as an example certain events in the recent history of theological education in Aotearoa-New Zealand, my intention is not to find a pretext either for relating personal experience or, indeed, for criticising the Church – of which I remain deeply fond, and among whose members are to be found my closest friends. Nor, indeed, is my intention to vent my frustration with those whose perspectives on theology and theological education are different from mine and whom I criticize in this article. It remains the case that I have learned a great deal from them, as should be clear from what follows, and I remain in their debt.

Consequently, I should like to dedicate this article not only to the very impressive students I was privileged to teach there, but also to those who worked so hard and gave so much in seeking to establish a programme of theological education which was worthy of the Church, true to its Lord and characterized by intellectual honesty and academic integrity. Finally, I should like to record my indebtedness to Dr Jeremy Begbie and Dr Francis Watson for their comments on an earlier draft of this chapter.

2. 'Aramoana' was the name of the sweeping beach and small settlement at the entrance to the Otago Harbour – described by the same colleague as 'the narrow neck of the womb in which we are all nourished'. The title 'Aramoana Christ' emerged, he explained, 'because for us God is earthed in this place, committed to the tangata whenua and the manuhiri of this harbour, clothed in the sparkling sands and white mists we all know and love so well' (Letter to the editor of the *Otago Daily Times*, 28th November 1990).

3. That same small settlement became the setting for one of the worst mass murders in Australasian history, which cost the lives of a dozen or so people, including several children, at the hands of a crazed gunman who was one of its residents. What soon became clear was that the 'Aramoana Christ' had absolutely nothing to say to the life struggles of the people there. The utilization of the label 'Christ' in this way amounted to the subjective expression and spiritualization of the romantic world-view of a few individuals.

As God-talk it was vacuous, reflecting the tragic failure to appreciate that it is neither sand nor sea that constitute a village, but rather its people – and that it is not God's being 'clothed in sparkling sands and white mists' that speaks of the divine commitment to the people of Aramoana but, rather, garments for which executioners threw lots and a head-piece which bore cruel testimony to the hideous evil of pointless and unwarranted violence and human cruelty. To replace the crucified Christ with the subjective associations deriving from picturesque locations is ultimately to deny any grounds for speaking of God's commitment to the world. It is God's unique and concrete self-identification as the crucified Christ that alone can speak of God's commitment to persons in and through the confusion, suffering and human tragedy that lurk behind outward appearances.

4. Gerald Patrick Fitzgerald, *Christ in the Culture of Aotearoa-New Zealand* (ed. Helen Bergin, Faculty of Theology, University of Otago, Dunedin, 1990). Dr Fitzgerald was simply articulating what others were advocating at the same time. The same colleague who had spoken of the 'Aramoana Christ' had suggested, in a widely-read Church monthly, that 'we have to give quality time to seeking to discern the Aotearoa Christ in the midst of Karangahape Rd and of the grand hills for sheep' (*Crosslink*, December 1990). The Faculty of Theology, which was responsible for publishing the book, was composed, in the main, of staff from the Theological Hall and Holy Cross seminary (the Roman Catholic college), who held honorary lectureships in the university.

5. In a similar vein, I heard it suggested that it was male envy of female menstruation that lay behind the utilization of blood in the eucharist.

6. 'Doctrine, Language and Imagery', in *Women and the Church* (ed. Chris Nichol), p. 19.

7. *Ibid.*, p. 23.

8. Enid Bennett, 'Sisterstory: Women as Saviour', in *With Heads Uncovered* (Women in Ministry Network, Auckland, 1988), pp. 48-49.

9. This was the Church committee responsible for the entire programme of theological education at the Hall.

10. As explained above, the Faculty of Theology in the university was largely constituted by the staff of the Theological Hall and Holy Cross Seminary. Most of the Hall's courses served as units of the theology degree offered by the university. The contribution of the Hall to the formation of the Faculty of Theology is recounted in Ian Breward, *Grace and Truth: A History of Theological Hall, Knox College, Dunedin 1876-1975* (Theological Education Committee, Presbyterian Church of New Zealand, 1975), pp. 169-76.

11. 'Junia... Outstanding Among the Apostles (Romans 16:7)', in L. and A. Swidler (eds.), *Women Priests* (Paulist Press, New York, 1977), pp. 141-44. Cited in Helen Bergin, Judith McKinlay and Sarah Mitchell, 'Sexism Ancient and Modern: Turning the Male World Upside Down' (*Pacifica* 3, 1990), pp. 158-59.

12. These insights are taken to their extreme in the 'post-modernist' emphasis on the reality-constituting character of language as expressed, for example, by Jacques Derrida. His approach finds expression in his book, *Of Grammatology* (Johns Hopkins University Press, Baltimore, 1976). For a lucid exposition of Derrida's views, see John Llewelyn, *Derrida on the Threshold of Sense* (Macmillan, Basingstoke, 1986). Theological parallels are to be found in Don Cupitt's *Creation Out of Nothing* (SCM, London, 1990).

13. Elizabeth Wilson and Sik Hung Ng, 'Sex Bias in Visual Images Evoked by Generics: A New Zealand Study' in *Sex Roles*, 18, 1988), pp. 159-68.

14. Helen Bergin, Judith McKinlay and Sarah Mitchell, *op. cit.*, p. 164.

15. It is relevant to note here that there is a highly significant non-parallelism here. In the case of the Otago study referred to, 'he' is being used of students (i.e. human beings), who are invariably gendered beings, whereas in the theological context the referent is 'God' who ought to be recognized by educated Christians to be beyond gender. The whole thrust of Wittgenstein's arguments, to which we refer, is to suggest that meanings are not 'fixed' for all contexts. Consequently, a word does not carry identical psychological associations in all contexts of its use, as this argument assumes. The meaning and rules of use applying to the pronoun 'he' when used of God are clearly different from those that apply when the pronoun is used of the non-human. This applies as much to the English language as it does to the various other European languages (e.g. French and German) which use 'gendered' pronouns of non-human referents and where this clearly does *not* involve

gender-projection on the part of the users. The French do not regard houses as female!

16. In the Greek of Galatians 3:28, the phrase is 'male *and* female', alluding to the creation narrative.

17. *Op. cit.*, p. 170. I would add that some of the preceding arguments above are borrowed from this same article.

18. Gavin D'Costa, 'The Impossibility of a Pluralist View of Religions', *Religious Studies*, 32, 1996), p. 224. In this section, I am utilizing D'Costa's helpful definitions of 'pluralism' and 'inclusivism'. For a more extended discussion of these issues, see my chapter, 'Inclusive Ministry and the Logical Impossibility of Theological Inclusivism, Pluralism and Relativism', in *The Call to Serve: Biblical and Theological Perspectives on Ministry in Honour of Bishop Penny Jamieson*, ed. Douglas A. Campbell (Sheffield Academic Press, Sheffield, 1996), p. 256-68.

19. *Ibid.*

20. *Ibid.*, p. 225. D'Costa opens his paper (which was originally presented to the Conference on Religious Pluralism, sponsored by the Centre for Philosophical Studies, King's College, London, on 25th February 1995), with a statement of impressive academic integrity in which he refutes the typology which he himself had done so much to promulgate over the previous eight years and which he had advocated in his profoundly influential book. He writes: 'This paper could be an act of public self-humiliation as in what follows I am going to suggest that a typology that I have promoted and defended against critics I now come to recognise as redundant' (p. 223).

21. *Ibid.*, p. 232.

22. I am borrowing an expression here from D.C. Williams's article, 'The Myth of Passage', *The Journal of Philosophy* (Vol. XLVIII, No. 15, 1951), pp. 457-72.

23. It is also no coincidence that the person who succeeded me in the chair of theology in Knox Theological Hall was a pupil of Don

Cupitt and eager advocate of a 'non-realist' position. Indeed, the 'non-realist' approach which he adopted in parish ministry was praised by Cupitt in the British press. In an article in the *Guardian* (10th December 1994) he wrote, 'I know a parish in New Zealand which has produced its own hymn-book of non-realist hymns. It is the most-nearly up-to-date parish Church in the world. They draw up their own services, and have voted out forms of words they feel we can no longer use honestly. You can worship there and say nothing untrue.' Cupitt goes on to argue that realist theologians are actually involved in worshipping Satan. 'And here is a curious fact... non-realism has perhaps never quite dared openly and explicitly to identify the god of the realists. Dare we say who he is?... But somehow, one can't quite say it out loud. The truth in this matter is just too fearful. But, in a moment of ecstasy, Jesus saw his fall. Do you read me?' In sum, the new orthodoxy of post-modernist theology is 'non-realism' or 'anti-realism', and its 'realist' opponents are now to be regarded as heterodox and anathematized accordingly as demonic.

24. This option, like every other, is an exclusive one – exclusive, that is, of contrary truth claims but *for the sake of* the inclusivism internal to these claims!

25. *Kulturprotestantismus* was the simple identification of Protestant Christianity with German culture manifest in theological circles during the period leading up to the First World War. In August 1914, a group of ninety-three German intellectuals, including several leading theologians, signed a declaration in support of the Kaiser's war policy. Their attitude, as Alasdair Heron points out, was that the Kaiser's war policy was 'necessary to the defence of Christian civilization'. See *A Century of Protestant Theology* (Lutterworth, Guildford), p. 75.

26. These were Germans who sought, during the 1930s, to wed their religious conviction with their commitment to national socialism and loyalty to Hitler. Christianity and the nature of the Church were thus reinterpreted in terms of a quasi-religious ideology of

'blood and soil' (*ibid.*, p. 86). One could also refer to a parallel dynamic in Fiji, where the devoutly Methodist, 'indigenous' population took power by force, repudiating the democratic, majority decision of the people and denying the political rights of the Indian Fijian population.

27. *Saeculum* in the Vulgate.

Notes to Chapter 7
The Virgin Mary and Other Women

1. The concept of 'harm' is itself problematical. Within a particular society, a given practice might maintain the continuity of the group concerned, and thus ensure the survival of both its female and male members. Seen from a more critical perspective, however, the practice might be judged to be harmful for women, and the society itself would then be judged to be in need of reconstruction, so that its survival would no longer be dependent upon a practice of such a kind. For the purposes of the present paper, I have not addressed this question directly.

2. Ratzinger, Cardinal Josef, (trans. John H.McDermott), *Daughter Zion: Meditations on the Church's Marian Belief* (Ignatius Press, San Francisco, 1983), p. 65.

3. Some studies which include relevant information on this subject are: Evelyn P. Stevens, 'Marianismo: The Other Face of Machismo in Latin America', in Ann Pescatell (ed.), *Male and Female in Latin America* (University of Pittsburgh Press), pp. 90-100; Campbell, Ena, 'The Virgin of Guadalupe and the Female Self-Image: A Mexican Case History', in James J. Preston, *Mother Worship: Themes and Variations* (University of North Carolina Press), pp. 5-24; Mitchell, Timothy, *Passional Culture: Emotion, Religion and Society in Southern Spain* (University of Pennsylvania Press, Philadelphia, 1990); Roussou, Maria, 'War in Cyprus: Patriarchy and the Penelope Myth', in Ridd, Rosemary, and Callaway, Helen (eds.), *Caught Up in Conflict: Women's Responses to Political Strife*

(Macmillan Education, Basingstoke, 1986), pp. 25-44. All these works concern Hispanic or Mediterranean cultures, and discuss how Marian devotion operates within these particular environments.

4. Daly, Mary, *Gyn/Ecology: The Metaethics of Radical Feminism* (Beacon Press, Boston, 1978).

5. Armstrong, Karen, *The Gospel According to Woman: Christianity's Creation of the Sex War in the West* (Elm Tree Books, London, 1986), p. 73.

6. Justin Martyr, *Dialogue with Trypho*, 100, 4-5; English translation given in O'Carroll, Michael, *Theotokos: A Theological Encyclopedia of the Blessed Virgin Mary* (Dominican Publications, Dublin, 1982), p. 211. A recent feminist analysis of the Eve-Mary typology is Schirmer, Eva, *Eva-Maria: Rollenbilder von Mannern fur Frauen* (Burkhardthaus-Laetare, Offenbach, 1988).

7. The writings of the Church Fathers on this and other themes of this chapter are considered by Rosemary Radford Ruether in her paper 'Misogynism and Virginal Feminism in the Fathers of the Church', in Ruether, R.R. (ed.), *Religion and Sexism: Images of Woman in the Jewish and Christian Traditions* (Simon and Schuster, New York, 1974), pp. 150-83.

8. Daly, Mary, *Beyond God the Father: Towards a Philosophy of Women's Liberation* (The Women's Press, London, 1986), p. 81.

9. Warner, Marina, *Alone of All Her Sex: The Myth and the Cult of the Virgin Mary* (Quartet Books, London, 1978). The quote from Sedulius appears in *Paschale Carmen* Book 2, v.69. English translation given in Berselli, Constante, and Gharib, Giorgio, *In Praise of Mary: Hymns from the First Millennium of the Eastern and Western Churches* (St Paul Publications, Slough, 1981), p. 52. Warner's use of this quotation in fact takes it out of context.

10. Houselander, Caryll, *The Reed of God* (Sheed & Ward, London, 1944), p. 1.

11. von Speyr, Adrienne (trans. Nelson, E.A.), *Handmaid of the Lord* (Ignatius Press, San Francisco, original German, 1948).

12. de Montfort, Louis Marie Grignon, *La Traité de Vraie Devotion a la Saint Vierge* (Librarie Mariale, Pontchâteau, 1934). The work was composed at the beginning of the eighteenth century, but it was then lost and not recovered again until 1842. An English translation is published by the Montfort Press, Liverpool.

13. Duffy, Eamon, *What Catholics Believe about Mary* (CTS Publications, London, 1989), p. 21.

14. Thomas Aquinas, *Summa Theologiae* (Blackfriars, with Eyre & Spottiswoode, London, 1963), 1a Q. 93, Art. 5, Vol. 13, p. 61.

15. *Ibid.*, 1a Q. 15, Art. 3, Vol. 8, p. 71.

16. *Ibid.*, 2a2ae Q. 26, Art. 10, Vol. 32, p. 149.

17. Gilson, Etienne, *History of Christian Philosophy in the Middle Ages* (Sheed & Ward, London, 1980), p. 298.

18. Mitchell, Timothy, *Passional Culture: Emotion, Religion and Society in Southern Spain*, p. 27.

19. Ranke-Heinemann, Ute, *Eunuchs for the Kingdom of Heaven* (Penguin Books, Harmondsworth, 1990), p. 342.

20. Harris, Marguerite Tjäder (ed.), trans. Kezel, Albert Ryle, *Birgitta: Life and Selected Revelations* (Paulist Press, New York and Mahwah, 1990), pp. 203-204.

21. *Ibid.*, p. 76.

22. McNeill, F. Marian, *The Silver Bough: A Four Volume Study of the National and Local Festivals of Scotland*, Vol. 1, *Scottish Folklore and Folk-Belief* (William McLellan, Glasgow, 1957), p. 75.

23. *Ibid.*, p. 175.

24. One version of this story is given in Herolt, Johannes, trans. C.C. Swinton Bland, *Miracles of the Blessed Virgin Mary* (George Routledge & Sons Ltd., London, 1928), pp. 43-45.

25. *The Prayers and Meditations of St Anselm* (trans. Sister Benedicta Ward, SLG) 'Prayer to St Mary (3)', 152-63 (Penguin Books, Harmondsworth, 1973), pp. 119-20.

26. Stauffer, Ethelbert (trans. Marsh, John), *New Testament Theology* (SCM Press, London, 1955), p. 118.

27. Miegge, Giovanni (trans. Smith, Waldo), *The Virgin Mary: The Roman Catholic Marian Doctrine* (Lutterworth Press, London, 1955), p. 30.

28. Brown, Raymond, *The Birth of the Messiah* (Geoffrey Chapman, London, 1993), p. 298.

29. *Ibid.*, p. 299.

30. *Ibid.*, p. 314. The Mariologist, René Laurentin, had previously given support to the view that Luke's Annunciation narrative is intended to be an account of a New Creation. See Laurentin, René, *Court Traité sur la Vierge Marie* (Lethielleux, Paris, 1968), pp. 137-38.

31. Newman, Barbara, *Sister of Wisdom: St Hildegard's Theology of the Feminine* (Scolar Press, Aldershot, 1987), p. 275; English trans. p. 163.

32. *De Glorificatione Trinitatis*, IX.6, PL169: 186d. Translation by Newman, Barbara, *op. cit.*, pp. 190-91.

33. White Jr., Lynn, *Medieval Technology and Social Change* (Clarendon Press, Oxford, 1962), p. 52.

34. White Jr., Lynn, *Medieval Religion and Technology: Collected Essays* (University of California Press, Berkeley, Los Angeles and London, 1978), p. 145.

35. Merchant, Carolyn, *The Death of Nature: Women, Ecology and the Scientific Revolution* (Wildwood House, London, 1982).

36. The Latin text is:

Quem terra, pontus, aethera
colunt, adorant, praedicant
trinam regentem machinam,
claustrum Mariae baiulat.

It probably dates from the ninth century. The most popular English translation is J.M. Neale's:

The God whom earth, and sea, and sky,
Adore, and laud, and magnify,
Who o'er their threefold fabric reigns,
The Virgin's spotless womb contains.

37. The view of Mary as an impossible model in itself seems to show some of the ways in which her cult has been affected by modernity. The principal motivation for the veneration of saints has hardly ever been a desire to imitate them: rather, people value them for their intercessory power. Official Church authorities have frequently tried to inculcate in their flocks the imitation of worthy examples, but the extent to which this has been successful is highly dubious. The fact that modern women have had the idea of Mary as a model impressed upon them so forcibly may perhaps be a consequence of the fact that with modern means of communication, the ideas of the hierarchy can be transmitted to the faithful far more efficiently than was previously the case.

Furthermore, the generally mechanized character of modern life gives people far less time for reflection upon the messages which they receive. This means that people have correspondingly less power to manage those messages in their own interests. The fact that rationalized cultures do not have much truck with miracles may also be a factor to be taken into consideration here. Women will not see Mary as a miraculous helper if they do not believe in the possibility of miracles in the first place!

However, my own conversations with a man from Ireland and a woman who has visited Nicaragua suggest that in both these places, women perceive Mary to be a sympathetic figure because she is a mother who suffered great anguish. My Irish informant was of the opinion that it is generally believed in Ireland that 'to be a mother is to suffer'. The visitor to Nicaragua said that a large number of women there have had adult sons who have been wrongfully executed, as Mary's son was at the Crucifixion. In these instances, then, it is not miraculous help which Mary supplies, but a figure who can share the woman's own grief or sorrow.

Notes to Chapter 8
Collective National Guilt

1. It seems to me that the Queen's action in relation to the Treaty of Waitangi is, in principle, the same as Chancellor Kohl's repudiation of the acts of Germans under the Nazi regime with respect to the holocaust. Symbolic gestures of this kind are appreciated. In such cases, there are relatively few intervening factors and third parties, and there is a simple moral asymmetry of a very grave kind to be recognized, together with consequences for the living susceptible to reparation. As indicated in the main text, such situations are relatively rare and cannot involve the notions either of collective guilt automatically incurred by membership in the nation, or collective guilt transferred across the generations.

If I were asked the question about Nelson Mandela's symbolic gesture of forgiveness to the white community, I would understand it as making sense in relation to those who in any way morally colluded with the premises on which the apartheid regime was based. Though such people would be numerous, they could not be defined in terms of colour. Moreover, Nelson Mandela has retained in principle the distinction between innocent and culpable to the extent that those guilty of crimes are to be charged and tried. They are not, of course, all of those who are guilty.

Notes to Chapter 9
Towards an Executive Church

1. In fairness to the Church Commissioners, it is important to note Sir Michael Colman's (First Church Estates Commissioner) observation in a press release from May 1996 that: 'A total return of 19.5% on the Commissioners' investments and an increase in value of over £300 million to £2.7 billion continues the strengthening of the Church of England's historic assets.'

2. Thus I do not question the motivation of the originators of the Turnbull Report, but merely draw attention to the possible outcomes of policies which when enacted elsewhere have involved questionable consequences.

3. See Bishop Turnbull's letter in the February 1996 issue of *New Directions*. This was written in reply to Roberts, R.H., 'Towards an Executive Church?' (*New Directions*, January 1996).

4. There is, of course, an immensely complex background to the interconnection of Church and state. See Doe, Norman, *The Legal Framework of the Church of England* (Oxford University Press, Oxford, 1996), and Bursell, Rupert D.H., *Liturgy, Order and the Law* (Oxford University Press, Oxford, 1996).

5. My sources must of necessity remain anonymous. They are largely based on the correspondence evoked by public controversy and publicity. I have unsuccessfully attempted to persuade Professor Robin Gill of the University of Kent to send me draft papers relating to his plans for the introduction of rational accountability into the activities of intermediate, parish and sector clergy.

6. The recent adoption of psychometric testing, devised and administered by recruitment and assessment services, as a means of deselecting the verbally able and supplementing the somewhat intuitive approach used at clergy selection conferences, is an interesting example of this process of aggregation.

7. It so happens that there is a remarkable convergence between human resources management and spirituality and religiosity. Managers can now employ spiritual techniques learned from religious traditions which, ironically, may frequently have half-forgotten their own inheritance. See Roberts, R.H., 'Power and Empowerment: New Age Managers and the Dialectics of Modernity/ Postmodernity', in Roberts, R.H. (ed.), *Religion and the Transformations of Capitalism: Comparative Approaches* (Routledge, London, 1995), pp. 180-98.

8. See Ritzer, George, *The MacDonaldization of Society*.

9. Current efforts to elaborate and then enforce uniform standards of 'graduateness' upon each university subject area are indicative of the latest stage of this trend. Using an initial eightfold set of categories (including the precise measurement of such attributes as 'psycho-motor skills' and 'client focus') in the context of the likelihood of an imposed core curriculum, the funding councils will be able to secure uniform, quantifiable and predictable 'quality' (fitness to purpose) across the expanded tertiary sector. This is the natural corollary of the trend to establish line-management and undivided executive power. The implications for a Church venturing down a parallel path are considerable.

10. The reader is to assume that this refers to the sub-discipline of sociology known as 'organization theory'. See Clegg, Stewart (ed.), *Handbook of Organisation Theory* (Sage, London, 1996).

11. This image is borrowed from Gregory Dix's idea of the 'shape' of the liturgy. Dix argues for a persisting pattern of eucharistic worship, independent of any particular locus of jurisdiction that might weaken the authenticity of Anglican claims to validity of its orders. In effect, the question of such legitimacy is moved from the line of Petrine succession to the conformity of the pattern of a contemporary cultural practice with the *Gestalt* of its forebears. There are other parallels in *Working as One Body* which are reminiscent of this methodology. It avoids the difficulties of grounding authority in tradition, rather than functional efficacy.

12. *Working as One Body* (Church House Publishing, 1995), pp. xii, 4ff., and 2-4 respectively.

13. *Ibid.*, p. ix.

14. This is in the sense employed by David Harvey where he excoriates 'the condition of postmodernity' as embodying serious and comprehensive political intent. See *The Condition of Postmodernity* (Blackwell, Oxford, 1989).

15. A painful lesson has yet to be learned in Britain. It is interesting that the assimilation of the managerial paradigm and its ethos into the Church of England takes place at the moment that this ethos is being questioned. See, for example, Simon Caulkin's review of Robert Locke, *The Collapse of the American Management Mystique* (Oxford University Press, Oxford, 1996). Locke criticizes the adequacy of a managerialism which not only 'subjects those in the workplace to the authority of a professionally dominant and aggressive career elite', but which also 'defeats and undermines the goals of management: the delivery of well-being to all those connected with the firm'. Caulkin's review was published as 'Casts and Cults Who Cast a Managerial Spell', *The Observer*, 9th May 1996.

16. The full quotation is treated at length in context by Roberts, R.H., 'Religion and the "Enterprise Culture": the British Experience in the Thatcher Era (1979-1990)', *Social Compass* 39(1), 1992, pp.15-33.

17. The recent change in the law that permits companies to displace the cultural expression of children's and students' work by 'invading' the walls of schools and other educational organisations with commercial publicity is a recent example. An ecclesiastically self-inflicted instance was the controversial celebration of the role of the Midlands motor vehicle industry in Coventry Cathedral which involved driving a car down the central aisle as part of the liturgy.

18. For a recent example, see Revel, Lynn, 'The return of the Sacred', in Wolton, Suke (ed.), *Marxism, Mysticism and Modern Theory*, (Macmillan, London, 1996), pp. 111-31. Revel writes (and surely this is full of potential implications for Christians and theologians): 'The self may have become God but it is an isolated and lonely self, limited by the fragmentary nature of its own parochial experiences and dreams, and impoverished by its inability to communicate with any other soul than its own,' (p. 131). For a full account, see Paul Heelas's forthcoming *The New Age Movement* (Blackwell, Oxford).

19. It is at such a juncture that the feminist rejection in principle of transcendent 'otherness' as a male construct deprives such theology from the power of resisting all malignant powers other than the oppression of men. The menace of managerialism lies in part (in particular, in its so-called 'postmodern' or post-Fordist forms) in its 'feminine' quality of non-objectification. In other words, really effective post-Fordist management is not the replication of Max Weber's famous 'steel-hard casing' or 'jacket' (*ein stahlhartes Gehause*, freely translated by Talcott Parson as the famous 'iron cage') but like a garment that fits so closely that we may fail to notice its existence until we find that it has become a skin-tight armour that dictates our flexions. See Weber, Max, *Die protestantische Ethik und der 'Geist' des Kapitalismus* (Athenaum, Hain Hanstein, 1993), p. 153.

20. There is much to be learned by the theologian and priest from Pierre Bourdieu's concept of 'critical reflexivity'. See Bourdieu, Pierre, and Wacquant, Loic J.D., *An Invitation to Reflexive Sociology* (University of Chicago Press, 1992).

21. For introductory background, see Jeavons, Thomas H., *When the Bottom Line is Faithfulness: Management of Christian Service Organisations* (Indiana University Press, Bloomington, 1994); Rudge, Peter, *Ministry and Management* (Tavistock, London); Sievers, Burkard, *Work, Death and Life Itself: Essays on Management and Organization* (Walter de Gruyter, Berlin, 1994); and the special issue on Ecclesiology and the Culture of Management, *Modern Theology*, 9/4, October 1993.

22. On the learning organization, see, for example, Honey, P., and Mumford, Alan, *The Manual of Learning Styles* (Honey, Maidenhead, 1986); Knowles. M., *Self Directed Learning* (Follett, Chicago, 1975); Kolb, D., *The Learning Style Inventory* (McBer and Co, Boston, 1976); Kolb, D., *Experiential Learning* (Prentice-Hall, New York, 1984); Revans, R.W., *Action Learning* (Bloud & Briggs, London, 1980).

23. *Working as One Body*, p. 4.

24. Max Weber's classic discussion of this conception is to be found in Roth, Guenther, and Wittich, Claus (eds.), *Economy and Society* (University of California Press, Berkeley, 1978), Vol. I, chapter IV, sections iv and v.

25. Norman, Edward, *Church and Society in England, 1770-1970: a Historical Study* (Clarendon Press, Oxford, 1976).

26. It is interesting to recall that it was Burnham's *The Managerial Revolution* that had a powerful impact upon George Orwell immediately before he wrote his novel, *1984*. Orwell appreciated the totalitarian implications of the managed society. Thus his prophetic capacity is to be judged not so much by the application of his vision in *1984* to global Communism, but to the triumph of resurgent capitalism.

27. *Staying in the City: Faith in the City Ten Years On: A report by the Bishop's Advisory Group on Urban Priority Areas* (Church House Publishing, London, 1995).

28. As advocated by the Archbishop of Canterbury in his speech in the House of Lords on 5th July 1996.

29. For an account of Novak's conception of the role of Judaism and Christianity in a 'democratic capitalist' world order, see Roberts, R.H., 'The Spirit of Democratic Capitalism: A Critique of Michael Novak', in Davies, Jon, and Green, David (eds.), *God and the Marketplace: Essays on the Morality of Wealth Creation* (Institute of Economic Affairs, London), pp. 64-81.

Notes to Chapter 10
Jesus and the Thought Police

1. Miesel, Rick, cited by Kennedy, J.W., 'Hunting for Heresy' in *Christianity Today* (16th May 1994), p. 40.

2. Pelikan, J., *The Christian Tradition: a History of the Development of Doctrine*, Vol. 1: *The Emergence of the Catholic Tradition (100-600)* (Chicago University Press, 1971), p. 69.

3. Jenson, R.W., *Story and Promise: a Brief Theology of the Gospel About Jesus* (Fortress Press, Philadelphia, 1973), p. 177.

4. Cumbey, C.E., *The Hidden Dangers of the Rainbow: the New Age Movement and Our Coming Age of Barbarism* (Huntington House, Shreveport, 1983), p. 168.

5. Wilkinson, L., 'New Age, New Consciousness, and the New Creation', in Granberg-Michaelson, W. (ed.), *Tending the Garden: Essays on the Gospel and the Earth* (Eerdmans, Grand Rapids, 1987), p. 222.

6. Passantino, B. and G., *Witch Hunt* (Thomas Nelson, Nashville, 1990), pp. 203-15, 220-27.

7. Alves, R A, *Protestantism and Repression: a Brazilian Case Study* (SCM, London, 1985).

8. *Ibid.*, p. 83.

9. Barth, K, *Church Dogmatics*, Volume I, Part 2 (T&T Clark, Edinburgh, 1956), p. 811.

10. 'The Barmen Declaration', translated by Cochrane, A.C., in Locke, H.G. (ed.), *The Church Confronts the Nazis: Barmen Then and Now* (Edwin Mellen Press, Toronto, 1984), pp. 19-26.

Contributors

Dr Andrew Walker is Senior Lecturer in Theology and Education at King's College, London. He is the author of several books, including *Restoring the Kingdom: The Radical Christianity of the House Church Movement* (Hodder & Stoughton, 1988), and *Telling the Story: Gospel, Mission and Culture* (SPCK, 1996).

Rev. Canon Martin Reardon is the General Secretary of The Churches Together in England. Canon Reardon has spent many years in ecumenical work and among his several books are *What On Earth is the Church For?*

Dave Tomlinson is a Christian leader and convenor of Holy Joe's, an unconventional Christian church that meets in a pub. He is a former leader in the house church movement but is now a member of the Church of England. He is the author of the controversial and highly successful *The Post-evangelical* (Triangle, 1995).

Steve Hunt is a lecturer in Sociology at Reading University, specializing in the sociology of charismatic movements. He is co-editor with Dr Malcolm Hamilton of *The Charismatics: Sociological and Religious Perspectives* (Macmillian, forthcoming).

Rev. Russ Parker is Director of the Acorn Christian Healing Trust. His publications include *Healing Dreams* (Triangle) and *Forgiveness is Healing* (DLT).

Julius H. Rubin is Professor of Sociology at St Joseph College, West Hartford, Connecticut. He is the author of *Religious Melancholy and Protestant Experience in America* (Oxford

University Press, 1994), and the forthcoming study, *The Other Side of Joy: Religious Melancholy Among the Bruderhof*. Both works are interdisciplinary investigations of the relationship between the Protestant ethic, evangelical conversion and psychological depression.

Dr Alan Torrance is Senior Lecturer in Systematic Theology at King's College, London, and the Director of the Institute of Systematic Theology. Previously he taught in the Universities of Otago, Aberdeen and Erlangen. He is the author of *Persons in Communion: An Essay on Trinitarian Description and Human Participation* (T&T Clark, 1996).

Sarah Jane Boss is Director of the Marian Studies Centre at LSU College of Higher Education, Southampton.

David Martin is Emeritus Professor of Sociology at London University (LSE) and is Honorary Professor at Lancaster University in the Department of Religious Studies. He is the author of many books, the latest being *Forbidden Revolutions: Pentecostalism in Latin America and Catholicism in Eastern Europe* (SPCK 1996).

Richard H. Roberts, formerly Professor of Divinity at the University of St Andrews, now holds a chair of religious studies at the University of Lancaster. He has published works on Ernst Bloch and Karl Barth, and edited collections on rhetoric and the human sciences, and religion and the transformations of contemporary capitalism.

Lawrence Osborn is a theologian currently based at Ridley Hall, Cambridge. His research interests focus on the place of the Christian faith in postmodern culture. His publications include *Angels of Light? The Challenge of the New Age* (DLT, 1992) and *Restoring the Vision: the Gospel and Modern Culture* (Mowbray, 1995).